I Almost Lost My Marbles

...Until I Didn't

Dorri Warga

I Almost Lost My Marbles
…Until I Didn't

Dorri Warga

WIFE & MOTHER | AUTHOR | RESILIENCE COACH

 Daring to Share Global

Published by D.R. Warga Publishing
July 2021 9781777774707

Copyright © 2021 by Dorri Warga
All rights reserved. No part of this publication may be reproduced, stored in or introduced into a retrieval system, or transmitted, in any form, or by any means (electronic, mechanical, photocopying, recording or otherwise) without the prior written permission of the publisher. This book is sold subject to the condition that it shall not, by way of trade or otherwise, be lent, resold, hired out, or otherwise circulated without the publisher's prior consent in any form of binding or cover other than that in which it is published and without a similar condition including this condition being imposed on the subsequent purchaser.

Editor: Diana Reyers
Typeset: Greg Salisbury
Book Cover Design: Olli Vidal

DISCLAIMER: Readers of this publication agree that neither Dorri Warga, nor Diana Reyers, or Daring to Share Global will be held responsible or liable for damages that may be alleged as resulting directly or indirectly from the use of this publication. Neither the lead publisher nor the self-publishing author can be held accountable for the information provided by, or actions, resulting from, accessing these resources.

I dedicate
"I Almost Lost My Marbles...Until I Didn't"
to anyone moving through one of
life's many challenges
and feel they don't know their way out.

I once felt that way, yet I found
that storms can regenerate us with new purpose.

It is my hope that you find the warrior within
and push through the dark days until
light and purpose present themselves to you.

~Dorri Warga

A portion of the profits from the sale of this book
will be donated to organizations supporting those in need.

Praise

*I Almost Lost My Marbles…Until I Didn't
is a story of emotional and physical survival.*

It is a realistic tale that mirrors what so many experience within the perils of single parenting, chronic illness, and the loss of a child. Dorri Warga forged through each with the determination of a warrior while simultaneously searching for her soul's identity and discovering love along the way.

As I read each chapter, I was captivated by the tenacity this brilliant human being had, along with the humour she used as a sword to ward off her deepest, darkest demons in order to provide herself and her children the best possible chance within a world that kept serving her, what most would deem, impossible obstacles.

Dorri continues to survive, but even more significantly, she is a beacon of hope, shining a bright light as an advocate for those seeking the fortitude to fight through life's challenges to get to the other side, celebrating deserving victories of all that is wonderful in this world.

~ Diana Reyers
Founder of Daring to Share Global
Author | Editor | Publisher

Gratitude

*To my wonderful eight children, my wish is that you always know
how blessed I am to be your mother.
We stood apart from the rest of the world through
the good, bad, and the ugly times
and bore evidence that we were a force to be reckoned with.*

*It was not easy, yet we persevered with the love
that bound us together as a family,
which taught us to appreciate the simpler things in life.
I would not change us for a million stars in the sky.
My heart thanks you for being you.*

*My dearest husband, Drew,
you have been my Rock since the moment we met.
The calm we created is evidence of our love for each other.
I am sure there were many times when you thought to yourself,
"You have got to be kidding, you are losing your marbles",
but were wise enough not to say anything.*

*Together we can move mountains.
I love you.*

Gratitude

Catherine Ewing, I owe you.
You taught me to be strong and follow my heart,
allowing me to make sense of things that I perceived to have no
sense – to never let go of my dreams and recognize that my gifts
were worthy of sharing.
You believed in me even when I didn't.

To my awesome friend, John De Frietas,
the actual catalyst in encouraging me to write my life story.
Your inspiration and belief in me provided the courage to move
forward and delve into the complete unknown
with true confidence.
Thank you for having faith in me and making this story possible.

Diana Reyers, what can I say?
Throughout the process, having you as my writing coach
and supporting me to self-publish, made me feel cared for,
appreciated, and inspired me to put the best of me onto paper.
Your guidance was so on point.
I learned a lot, not just about writing,
but in becoming aware of my authentic self.
I feel I have made a friend, lovely lady.

Prologue
By Catherine Ewing

I am of the opinion that our brief *walk about* on this planet embodies so much more than we can comprehend. The tragedies we endure, the mistakes we make, the people who cross our path, the loss of a loved one, the shared laughter that leaves you gasping for breath, the pure joy of just being human — all of it makes for an incredible pallet of potentials. When we get out of our own way, the lessons are spectacular. THAT is what Dorri is all about.

When our paths first crossed and I learned that she had eight children, I was rendered speechless. Surely someone as seemingly bright as she was, knew what caused pregnancy...? She was breathing, upright and actually laughing about it, and although my immediate thought was to have her committed, I decided to give her a few days to prove me wrong. Glad I did...she not only proved me mistaken but became a trusted and loved part of my journey here. Her life lessons have been brutal at some points, the losses overwhelming but her growth incomprehensible.

Most humans do not start their day with thoughts of changing someone's world, and yet we may unknowingly hit a nerve that is the tipping point into a major shift in thinking, interacting, or life circumstance. I watched Dorri make such changes to lives daily, and she did it from her heart — always. It is what makes her...well, Dorri. In the midst of personal crises and eight children clamouring for her attention, she treated the immigrants who came through our doors as an extension of her family. She would not settle for just doing her job but always made sure that each individual was treated with respect and put on the path with the best long-term potentials for their particular skills.

I was blessed to work with her again within the environment of an indigenous community where she was doing employment development. Our roles were reversed with me, the contractor answering to her, the client. It made no difference to our relationship, and if anything, it flourished as we explored new possibilities together. Watching her confidence grow with each battle and success was inspiring and humbling. All of her experiences, losses, fears and triumphs came into play as she related to each situation she encountered with wisdom that can only be born from experience and heartfelt understanding. The core essence of what makes Dorri unique shone through brightly as she dealt with the difficulty of changing time-worn social norms within a close-knit community. The changes that she made endured <u>because</u> she wears her heart on her sleeve, and that wins hands down over *policy* every time.

Like water sculpts a beach with every wave, our daily lives have the potential to do the same to us. Dorri is the gentle, loving creature she is today because she walked through the fire and not only endured but allowed the scars to define her responses to those around her in the midst of their own fires. She has the compassion that comes from experience and the wisdom born of understanding those experiences.

> Life is about lessons, and for many, including myself, Dorri has been one of the greatest teachers.

Introduction
By Dorri Warga

Life is filled with moments of hope and opportunities to grow. Each of us has the chance to create our unique truth and insight through whatever circumstances present themselves. I know I did. I found lessons within both the good times and the not-so-good times. I was never afraid to fail and did not prolong my failures by allowing myself to get stuck in them. Instead, I discovered that I could reframe perceived failures into well-deserved gained knowledge to guide me forward in life.

This is my story, written with the hope that it resonates with and inspires my readers to recognize that their goals are within reach. It started as a memoir written to my children and then grew with new intentions. I decided to share my journey to support anyone going through life's challenges and encourage those feeling overwhelmed by the storms they face to dig deep and forge ahead.

My life has been an adventure with twists and turns that helped create my current reality of peace and balance. For me, this meant digging deep into my soul to find the warrior within. I was never stronger than when facing my fears head-on; it was then when I became genuine in both heart and soul. I saw beyond the boundaries that fear sought to bind me, and I found my worth. They say many people walk into your world, but only special ones leave footprints that help shape us for years to come — my story has countless heroes.

Our mistakes don't define us. What defines who we are is our ability to learn from our mistakes. We take risks and challenge ourselves by looking ahead at what awaits us. This takes motivation, resilience, and the perception that you can and will succeed.

The title of my book, *I Almost Lost My Marbles...Until I Didn't*, represents the overwhelm I felt through many storms, as well as the victories that make up my life story. I often thought I had completely lost my marbles only to pick them up, seeing them presented as completely new and brilliant colours. I humbly wish the same for you; you can accept your authentic self with the joy that I did and know that what you imagine can be achieved.

I allowed myself to look inward, to be vulnerable and accept change. The change was what I needed in order to contribute to the world uniquely. I needed to know who I am in all my authenticity – to be who I am without apologizing. When I discovered what works for me in my world and what doesn't, I became a catalyst for change. I fully believe that the universe knows what we need and when we need it, and life has a miraculous way of placing these incredible opportunities before us. All we need to do is reach out and use them to become who we are from within. Oh, and sometimes, you have to go a little crazy to stay sane.

I Almost Lost My Marbles
…Until I didn't

I

Turning My Deepest Pain into Understanding

Even if I could have seen it coming, I could not have prepared myself for what entered my life in 2010. Within that time, I could actually feel my heart breaking into a million pieces, causing me to doubt if I could possibly go on. I lost my son Nicholas to a drug overdose — his death was sudden and extremely painful, not only for me but for our entire family.

My oldest daughter called me early one morning with the phone call no mother ever wants to receive. She was crying, *Mom, Nic is in the hospital with a drug overdose and isn't expected to make it; come now.* I was living on Vancouver Island, British Columbia and he was in the intensive care unit on the mainland in Richmond. I kept begging my husband, Drew, to tell me Nic was going to be alright, but he couldn't. Because Drew would never lie to me, I knew it probably wasn't going to end well. I was numb all the way to the airport. I did not cry. I experienced no real feelings, being in a daze of sorts, trying to wrap my head around what was transpiring. Throughout the whole flight to get to my son, I kept hoping against hope that everything would be alright when I got there.

One of his best friends and my middle daughter met me at the airport; I could tell by their faces that, indeed, everything was not ok. His friend asked me if I needed anything before we got to the hospital, and I remember we drove through a drive-through. I ate what was to be my last meal for several days, not tasting anything and breaking down with my daughter's arms around me. We were all crying as we left for the hospital, which was ten minutes away.

Nicholas's addiction journey began after a car accident and having been prescribed OxyContin for pain. He was hooked. After the doctors would not prescribe it anymore, he went through the back-door dealers. His sisters and I tried to persuade him to go to rehab, but he refused to even look at a private facility when my oldest daughter offered to sell her expensive car to pay for it. Nic did not budge in his belief that he could recover by himself. That in itself showed he needed help. Yet, I never once foresaw this to the end with him *passing away way too soon in his young life*. Those words brought on a whole new meaning to me.

When I arrived in the ICU waiting room, so many of Nic's friends were gathered there. The room was filled even though only immediate family was allowed. My son was loved by so many. Nic had a heart of gold, and despite the different path he stumbled upon, they were there because they all loved him. Many of these friends call me Mom - and still do. It was a blessing to have them there, surrounding us with their love for Nic. The nurses deviated from the rule and told me what a beautiful family I had - all 18 of them - and left it at that. Their compassion was genuine and appreciated. I will always treasure that each of Nicholas's friends could go in and say goodbye to him.

I remember going into his hospital room and watching his lifeless body lying there. The doctors had put him into an induced coma. Every once in a while, he would reach his fingers out, and I thought, *He isn't dying; he hears me.* I ran to the nurse's station full of hope, but they just looked at me with sadness in their eyes and encouraged me to keep speaking to him. After performing a cat scan on him, the doctor came in and told our family that he only had ten percent brain function. The only thing keeping my son alive was a life support machine, and he asked me for permission to take him off.

He prefaced this, asking me if donating his organs was an option. It was all so overwhelming that I didn't have an answer right away. He added that time was limited in order to harvest his organs. I lost it! I completely and totally lost it! Screaming at him, I questioned why I would entrust him with my son's organs if he wasn't good enough to save my son. I ran out of the room and sat outside on a stretcher reduced to a crumpled-up ball. My soul searched to understand what was happening.

A couple of young men I didn't know came to my side. One of them put his arms around me and held me as I wept. My mind was not clear, being in so much pain. I cannot describe this gut-wrenching type of pain; there are simply no words. A social worker came out and introduced herself and asked me if I wanted to go to the chapel with her. I was so angry at God at that moment that I practically screamed at her, answering, *Why would I do that?* She backed off fast.

Eventually, I went in and gave the doctor permission to take Nic off the life support machine. Nicholas was firm in his belief in helping others. I did not think my athletically proud son would want to be kept alive by machines. I asked for a minister to come into Nic's room while we, his family, said goodbye. I know that didn't make any sense given my reaction to the social worker, but my son had a spiritual side to him that I thought needed to be honoured.

I could not watch him pass away. I am grateful to this day that my ex-husband was able to stand by our son's side as he took his last breath. The fact that he did not pass away alone is comforting.

My son was my hero, and he struggled with addiction for

many years, but he was my son first, and addiction was only a part of him. Nicholas was my little boy who had a loving heart and had my back no matter what. He was extremely sensitive and the one who shovelled snow for others all Christmas Eve in order to buy me a Christmas present. Addiction led him to his death at the age of 28. As I write this in honour of him, tears flow from my eyes and creep down my cheeks. This is definitely the most painful experience of my life – the pain never subsides.

I signed the donor card that allowed his organs to be harvested; they found recipients for his lungs, kidneys, eyes and liver. At first, this was not a comfort to me. I was angry that my son was not here.

> ***Why should others have my son's organs while I could no longer have my son.***

It was an irrational thought and a very confusing time for me. I was angry at the world, a world within which my son would never be with me again. However, I knew that even though Nic had never signed a donor card, he always gave freely to others. He did not die in vain. My conflicting emotions ran so raw and were all-consuming.

Our family attended a service honouring organ donors, and I felt like a fraud. Part of this was triggered by the guilt I accepted as the parent who allowed him to take his last breath without me. My feelings of deception also came from wanting my son back so much — I was not thinking rationally. The pain felt by each of my seven remaining children was deep and outwardly expressed in ways that were as unique as they are. Some were angry. Some felt guilty. All were incredibly sad. We all recognized that we had the right to our individual responses, and no one judged the other. I was so proud of them, and I tried my best to be strong for them, but they understood my pain. We took his ashes to the bar he often frequented. His picture was posted on their wall as it was his favourite spot. We knew he was well-loved in the community and heard how he would sit with someone who appeared lonely and sad to listen to their stories. That was my son.

His memorial was painful, and even though it was just a week after his passing, we held it in a funeral home. His father thought it was for the best, and I was so completely disconnected from reality I agreed. There were 144 people in attendance. The music I chose was *To Where you Are* by Josh Groban, *Amazing Grace* and *Rock of Ages*. His Dad chose Bob Seger's *Like a Rock*. I walked out to the main room in the funeral home to Josh Groban's *To Where you Are* and thought, *This cannot be real*. I kept looking behind me at a sea of faces searching for what I do not know - just searching. My gaze met a crowd of people crying; this spoke to the finality of what had transpired. I think I was trying to make sense of what was happening, using my eyes to plead with someone, anyone, to tell me this was all a bad dream. What I saw through my tears as I looked around was the amazing number of people who came to honour him on such short notice. There was such an outpouring of love from his friends. My oldest son wrote and read the eulogy while each of my other children said a few words. Nicholas was loved and well-respected in the community. His football coach from high school and his grade 12 teacher were there. They saw the obituary in the newspaper and were shocked. One of his friends got permission for us to receive Nic's football jersey.

On his birthday the following April, we scattered his ashes in the Fraser River at a dock where he and my oldest son and daughter often went to party. Then, friends and family went back to the house to write messages on balloons and release them to send him off. I took some of his ashes back to the island with me, taking him out on our boat to lay him to rest in the quiet calm waters where he last swam with us. Drew, I, and my youngest daughter spread some of his ashes in the River. I smiled and threw him a cigarette as he was always bumming one from me. I spoke out loud, *One last time Nic, one last time.*

I had to grieve separately. I needed the space and comfort of our boat tied up at the harbour on Vancouver Island. Over the years, the ocean became my safe place. And I needed my Drew. As always, my loving husband was there, and he instinctively knew what to do. He allowed me to weep. I can't say cry because it was more than that with a raw and deep pain needing to be released. The degree of pain was crippling to the point where there were moments I thought I had lost my marbles. Drew watched as I emptied my heart completely of the love I could no longer give. After I finished, he would come over and hug me. He held me, telling me it would be alright, and he reassured me I was doing what I needed to do to survive.

For a long time, I blamed myself for taking Nicholas off life support. Deep within me, I knew he would not have wanted to live in a vegetative state - my son was athletic and strong with a huge heart. It took a long time for me to accept that I did a loving thing for him. The pain will always be with me, and I continue to cry ten years later. In my pain-filled place at that time, I didn't want to be respected for making that decision. One day I shared how I truly felt with a very good friend, Carol. I told her that I could not help thinking that I killed him when I took Nicholas off life support. She lovingly replied,

Turning My Deepest Pain into Understanding

If God had wanted him to live, he would still be here.
God called him home; he is your angel now.

Those words gave me some semblance of peace.

If the drug dealers who moved his body away from where he collapsed stood before me, I would tell them that they stole precious minutes that could have prevented Nicholas's death. However, I will not allow them the ability to take away my memories, my peace, or my love for my son. Karma has its way of biting people in the butt, so I choose to let it be. My Nicholas will own a piece of my heart forever. I honour him by smiling through my tears, remembering his silly grin, his compassion for other humans, and so much more. I hold these close to my heart. It has taken over a decade to get to this point. Even still, I have days when something triggers a memory, and it brings me to my knees - a song, an expression, or a picture of him finds me frozen in grief.

Writing about Nicholas is challenging because while doing so, I feel his presence close to me; it's like he's sitting right by my side. Tears run out of my heart, missing my boy; *Sweet Feet* is what I called him. However, sharing this has helped me recognize that healing from his death may never be complete. I accept that. Losing my child created lifelong pain. It eases a little, but at any time, it can creep up like a tsunami crashing over me.

Nicholas came to me one day shortly after he passed. I was back on the island in a house we rented for the winter. I remember it like it was yesterday. I was sitting on the couch in front of the fireplace after a particularly difficult day, thinking about how much I missed my son and feeling guilty about taking him off life support. I couldn't have wept any harder as a raw gut-aching pain completely overtook my body, aching from my head to my toes. Drew was away at work, and it was the middle of a sunny afternoon. Extreme exhaustion overcame me, and being mid-afternoon with no one home, I decided to lie down in my bedroom. As I lay on my bed, I suddenly felt Nicholas's presence. To this day, I do not remember if he said anything to me, but I felt his arms around me as he rocked me to sleep. I don't know how long I slept, but when I woke, there was a light on in my bedroom, which only he could have turned on because it was daylight when I went to sleep and all the lights had been turned off. I think the best way to describe this is that I was surrounded by my son's peace. My pain was still there, but somehow, I knew that wherever my son was, he was now at peace.

I wished that I could allow myself that as well. I was haunted by unusual thoughts of the unknown. I wanted to know where he went; was he alright in heaven, or was he drifting around? I was used to him being with me in the present form, and it was unsettling, having no idea where his spirit was. I felt empty, yet I had to learn to accept this as my reality – this has been the roughest journey my soul has ever taken. But somehow, his coming to me that day was a gift that allowed me some sense of acceptance. I cannot commit to saying I have landed in peace because that is still an everyday struggle.

Experiencing the loss of my child is a profound process that has taken me through many stages - the first being shock and denial, which I experienced at the hospital. My head knew what my heart could not accept. My little boy was gone, and I could do nothing to change that. The pain was unbearable, and at times, my guilt within that final decision was overwhelming. I was angry - angry at God, the doctors, and even Nicholas for leaving me. I became depressed and played songs we used to listen to so that I could cry and get the pain out. I suppose I did not want to feel numb. I also longed to be alone, and yet, I felt the need to connect. This was where grief counselling came in. I needed to be around others who could identify and work through this storm with me. So, one day, seeking the hope of being with others who would understand, I picked up the telephone and called a grief counsellor where we lived.

Shortly after, I met with my grief counsellor, Michael. He used the term *accidental suicide* when I told him what had happened. Even though it applied to my son's death, I attributed his death to manslaughter, given whoever moved his body had stolen any chance of his life being saved. Michael was in the midst of forming a support group for mothers who had lost an adult child, and given my counselling experience, he asked me to join him and another mother to design that particular group. We met weekly for over two months, and my work there, both dealing with my own grief and supporting others, was very cathartic. I was humbled by the strength I saw and the real desire these women had to support one another while experiencing grief that often felt debilitating and misunderstood. It was healing, providing a hand up with my experiences. To be able to help other mothers understand the process with empathy and knowledge helped me make sense of my grief. Losing a child is a heavy storm. Once again, my healing evolved from my intention to learn to grow while helping others do the same. To this day, I have moments when a song, a picture, or simply a thought comes to me, and it brings me to my knees. Nicholas loved Johnny Cash, and *Ring of Fire* was one of his favourite songs. When I hear that song, I am thrown back into another day and time that included my son. Other times when listening to Kid Rock, I am reminded of being silly with him, rolling down the car windows while head-bumping to his songs.

Over the years after speaking to other mothers who lost a child, the common question that keeps me awake at night is *How do I go on without him?* I somehow managed to gain coping mechanisms to go through living my life without Nicholas in it - I continue to get *through* it, not *over* it. Most people who have not been in my shoes cannot understand. Some who do not know what I know say things to me without thinking. A piece of my heart was ripped out because I loved and was loved back by my precious child. I held his hand for the first time. I wiped his tears, hurt when he hurt and celebrated his victories alongside him. I keep my child in that special place.

Sharing my memories of him gives me some sort of peace, yet ironically, having peace is the most difficult part. Remembering Nicholas also means realizing he is not with me on this earth anymore. I have learned to smile at the thought of his silly ways, shake my head thinking of his stubbornness, and bring back some of the joy he brought into my life. It has been a journey - one of the most challenging roads I ever had to walk. I am gentle with my loved ones because they have, of course, lost as well. My children all grieved in their unique way, and I was so proud to see them respect their different responses to their brother's death. Even Drew who came into Nicholas's later into his life has special memories of him and copes in his own way.

I encouraged my friends to talk to me about my child. He existed, and even if they think I will be hurt by bringing up my child s name to me, Nicholas was and is part of my reality. As I told my children growing up, both my boys and girls, it's alright to cry. Tears are God's way of releasing the rain inside of us. I now know that the tears of grief are a sign of the love that cannot be shared here on earth.

I saw an eagle the other day, and it brought back memories of you. Missing my Sweet Feet, but I know you are on to better things. Always and forever missed. Soar like an eagle proud and free. May you be at peace and know that I keep you safe in my heart. Angel kisses until I can once more hold you in my arms.

Love Mama

My son's passing pushed me forward to understand more about addiction and perhaps make a difference. I did so in his honour and for all those struggling with addiction; they are someone's father, mother, brother, sister, and someone else's child. Addiction and homelessness are often the results of trauma, each as individual as the person going through these painful experiences. My other children did not turn to hard drugs and, like me, didn't understand the impact that a life of addiction made until we all experienced the aftereffects.

In May of 2012, I applied for and was successfully appointed to the coalition formed to assist those with addiction and homelessness by the mayor and council of the town where we harboured our yacht. The intention was to build low-barrier housing for those needing it.

At this time, Drew and I lived on our boat, and I was fortunate to have daily talks with those living in the homeless community who gathered every morning above our slips. They slowly built trust in me and spoke freely of their fears, addiction, and hopes for help. Many were Indigenous and spoke about addiction on the reservations. I remember telling one of the men about my son and my struggle to overcome feelings of guilt of not getting him into rehab before he passed. I will never forget his reply, *His journey was his and his alone. When drugs took over, there was nothing other than loving him through his bad days and good days that you could have done. I hope you do not blame yourself. You cannot force help; it had to be what he wanted.*

I told him that my son's friends said he had been clean for three months until that night. This man asked me if he could hug me. I agreed, and after the hug, he asked me to sit down beside him. With tears in his eyes, he said, *I lost my girlfriend a year ago. She had been in and out of rehab but was clean for a couple of months when she took drugs again and died that night. Her system couldn't take the drugs anymore.* I asked him what it would take to get him off the street. He looked me straight in the eye and said, *A home of my own away from the others who do drugs, so I can't be tempted – a place where I could get the help I need.* The conversations I had with this gentleman helped me let go of the guilt I held onto and gave me a new respect for those who cannot access the support they so desperately need.

Our coalition's purpose was to find funding for low barrier housing, which incorporates resources, both on and off-site, for its occupants. Ideally, a homeless person suffering from addiction can be housed even while still using but must possess a desire to move away from using drugs or alcohol. Individuals are provided with a safe and healthy alternative. The houses are staffed 24 hours a day by mental health counsellors and support staff.

There was some funding from Island Health, and we needed to obtain additional money to purchase the home and provide staffing for low barrier accommodation. This would, in turn, offer apartments in a more private setting than in a shelter with more easily accessible services for those who demonstrated a desire to get off the streets. The objective was to house those affected by mental health challenges and addiction issues. This would allow participants in the housing to have a firmer foundation than when living on the street with services pinpointed to their exact needs. It would provide a source of stability and care that they had been missing, some for years. Not all homeless people are addicts. This was a challenge I was up for.

I sat on the coalition with members from different agencies and societies that served the city's homeless population. Members of the coalition represented various mental health agencies, several churches, and community members. These participants all had a great deal of experience in the area of homelessness, much more than I did. I simply had the desire to help where I could. I was selected to represent the citizens of the town and was honest in my application, saying that although my son was never homeless, he had passed away from a drug overdose. I resonated with something shared by the Director of Mental Health. She nailed it when she compared addiction with the chicken-egg scenario, stating, *Which comes first, mental illness or addiction? For each person, it is different. One thing that is a commonality in this is that mental illness and addiction are all consuming, most often as a result of loss or trauma. Addicts turn to drugs or alcohol to ease the pain associated with the trauma. Most have experienced anxiety, depression, sexual abuse, PTSD, or isolation, just to name a few. They seek comfort away from their pain in substance abuse. There are adults who are wealthy businesspeople who use in the privacy of their homes often when alone. That is where overdoses occur most often. There are tainted drugs everywhere, and one does not know if they are getting clean drugs or not. Tainted drugs do not discriminate by income.* Although this is not word-for-word, the message resonated with me, and I must admit I learned a lot. Our challenge certainly wasn't a lack of ideas. I had my first taste of how politics can play a significant role in the inability to make a clear decision. Our committee members had diverse backgrounds and agendas, so there were many conversations related to how best serve their individual clientele rather than the community as a whole. The coalition met once a week to discuss how to implement low-barrier housing in the community and often got off track. The intent of how to best serve our homeless population took on a life of its own, which was understandable, but I did not feel effective in creating a clear plan for social housing. Because there are so many different reasons for a person living on the street, our approaches were often in conflict.

I learned a lot about those who were considered the *hidden homeless*. Among many, they included seniors who temporarily stay with family members, those on waiting lists for assisted living or rent-to-income apartments, men and women who couch surf because they cannot afford the added expense of utilities, as well as individuals working minimum wage jobs not able to secure housing or pay rent due to affordability. These people often accessed support through services such as crisis centers, women's shelters, and food banks. I learned of a family of three living out of their old van. They were parents who held minimum wage-paying jobs but did not get the hours needed to sustain apartment living. This was no way to bring up their child who was at real risk of being taken away from them through no fault of theirs. This made me so sad. Here were people choosing to work rather than accept government assistance yet had barely enough money to survive.

I learned there is often a perception in the community that all people living on the street are *worthless junkies* or *alcoholics*. Therefore, they did not want one of these housing units in their neighbourhood. I understand they have a right to their opinion, but the belief by many I spoke with was that every homeless person is dangerous. They are incorrect. Although they professed to understand the need for low-barrier apartments, their real concern was that their property values would go down, or their children might interact with who they addressed as *those people*. Indeed, some turn to crime to feed their addiction. I genuinely believe they are in a desperate situation and are the ones who possibly need help the most. But like all segments of humanity, they do not necessarily define the homeless population.

As a result of the lack of community support, one of our major roadblocks in developing low-barrier housing was finding its location. In order to appease the voters, even the mayor and council were often critical of the concept. They had been given the funds to endorse the coalition but lacked the foresight to back us. I never felt we had their full support. Most of the citizens preferred if the housing was in the country. However, that was not realistic as the services our clients needed to access were in town. Eight years later, I learned of a homeless man beaten to death in front of the Royal Bank in this same city. The man was not an addict but was homeless as a recent result of losing his home due to job loss. This was a direct result of the Covid-19 pandemic.

The cry for justice is out there. I spoke frankly about being on the coalition years ago, and the participants spoke again about the need for low-barrier housing. One person suggested a van to go around at night checking on the homeless and bringing them a warm drink and a sandwich. This initiative was done eight years ago. It appears not much has changed over the past few years to alleviate the homeless situation, and that breaks my heart.

It was very frustrating to sit there meeting after meeting and witness the downplay of a great idea into a political foray. Our coalition started to dwindle in size, and it was obvious to many that we did not have the support necessary to move forward. I was one of the members that ended up leaving. This experience left me with many more questions than answers. I wanted to make our goal come to fruition, but I saw the obstacles with my own eyes. I could not envision a way to make things work without the needed supports in place.

It was not all for not. A women's safe house was created, and more money went into developing winter shelters built out of shipping containers. However, they were only on loan for the winter months, so there was still no permanency for a person to access sustainable support. There is still much to do in supporting the homeless population with the opioid crisis, creating more loss of life in BC than the pandemic.

My heart goes out to all the mothers who have lost a child to addiction. I know first-hand the devasting pain that never heals. My only ask of others is to have some degree of compassion and understanding when seeing someone on the street who is under the influence. There are no easy answers, and in my opinion, mental health will continue to need more resources to curb the spread of this disease. Until one has walked in another's shoes, they have no right to judge –compassion is the gateway in finding a solution. It could happen to anyone, fellow human beings who have the right to be supported and respected. No one wakes up one day and decides they want to be homeless, and most of us cannot even begin to imagine the journey it took to take them there. Through different circumstances, anyone could find themselves without the support to survive.

Homelessness, addiction, and mental health run hand in hand. While my son was not homeless, he faced identical issues requiring acknowledgement and acceptance of help. Some will get help if offered, and some, like my son, never recover. It makes me sad when people turn away from those less fortunate and lump them all as unworthy criminals. Addiction is a disease just like cancer. I could never turn my back on my child if diagnosed with cancer. I know I could not.

I Almost Lost My Marbles...Until I Didn't

In honour of my precious son, Nicholas
Always in my heart... Never forgotten
April 1982-Oct 2010

II

The Beginning

In June 1953, I was born to Thelma and Paul Smith in a hospital in North York, Ontario. My mother passed away from heart and kidney complications a few months after my birth, and I was given to my aunt and uncle to raise me. They adopted me at an early age, and as a child of privilege, my life looked idyllic. In many parts, it was. However, the dark secret of my adoption left me feeling dirty, unworthy, and ashamed — I was never told I had a living biological father, so I thought Paul must be dead. He was never mentioned throughout my entire childhood - I fantasized he was a pilot and war hero killed in combat. If I imagined this to be true, I could understand him not being a part of my life. But deep down inside, I felt he did not want me, which was not unrealistic as it turned out. In later years as an adult, I blamed myself for my birth mother's death because I was told she should not have got pregnant due to other health issues she experienced. Ouch. I believed it was my fault that my mother died.

    I struggled alone with deep shame that grew into feelings of abandonment. There are those who may think I was unjustified to feel this way but growing up with everyone knowing the truth except for me was traumatizing. I wasn't officially told I was adopted until a friend of mine and I were swinging in the schoolyard. We were arguing, and she retaliated, *At least I'm not adopted!* I was shocked and went home to tell my parents. I was only about eight years old, and while sitting at the supper table, I turned to my father and asked him, *Are you not my real Daddy?* My father began to cry, got up from the table, and just left the room - this was a man who rarely showed his emotions. My mother looked at me and told me that I already knew I was adopted; *I told you when you were three.* Oh boy, what three-year-old comprehends that? I was told never to mention it again. The shame I experienced for making my father cry was overwhelming. I never mentioned my adoption again, keeping my emotions to myself. My parents never mentioned my biological parents for over four decades; I felt robbed of the ability to know who my birth mother was, only to hear later that she was much like me.

When I was 50, my adoptive mother finally said she wanted to talk to me about my biological mother, and it was a strange conversation indeed. She told me that Thelma loved to laugh, made people happy, and she wanted me very much. She also said she wished I had wanted to know more about my biological mom when I was younger. I just shook my head because there was never an invitation to discuss my adoptive parents when I was growing up. To this day, I am not sure what I missed during that conversation, but it certainly didn't provide the opportunity for me to learn more about why I was adopted. It seemed too late, and I felt she never understood, so I just left it there.

There were hints along the way that uncovered bits of my past; some were subtle, and some more poignant, like my friend's outburst on the swing set. For some reason, she knew about my adoption, but we never talked about it again until much later in life. In fact, I never talked about it to anyone; less because of being uncomfortable and more because I was confused and filled with the shame ingrained in me from when I questioned my father about it. There was such a level of secrecy around my adoption that I did not want to upset anyone, so I did not.

Then there were the times when the minister and his wife at the church we attended came to visit my parents' house. It was quite often, and I didn't know they were my biological grandparents at the time. Every visit with them left me feeling extremely uneasy as they hugged me too tight and brought gifts upon returning from their travels. My parents told me to call these people *Grandma and Grandpa Smith*, which was not that unusual, seeing as I addressed all my parents' friends using the surnames, aunt and uncle. One day, while at my best friend's house, I looked out their kitchen window and saw my Grandma and Grandpa Smith's car. I phoned home and told my mother that I would not come home until they left. Over time, I shared with my mother how awkward their visits felt, and I asked her to tell me when they were coming to visit, so I could plan to go to my friend's house. They never came after that. Their secret was still intact, and I was still left not knowing who they were or why they made me feel so uncomfortable. I felt a deep disconnect from everyone in my life.

> ***I questioned why I was so different from all my friends, yet I was afraid to ask who these people were or why they were always visiting us.***

One Mother's Day, one of the ladies at the church was giving out carnations at the door - you got a red one if your mother was alive and a white one if she had passed on. My mother took a white one for herself, and she gave me a red one. The woman giving out the flowers turned to my mother and said, *Bertha, she should be wearing a white one too*. My mother looked at her and said, *She is fine*. This upset me because I was confused, not knowing that my biological mother had passed away. I did not know this woman standing with me was not my natural mother. She turned to me and said, *You have the right flower*. What she didn't understand was that it wasn't about the flower. I wanted to know what that lady meant and how the words pained me, even if I didn't know why. I must have been six or seven at the time, and I never forgot this woman's confusing words and how unkind and hurtful they felt.

Throughout all of this, I never able to let go of my shame. Being responsible for an adult secret was a lot to ask of a little girl. The repercussions of seeing my father cry when I asked about my adoption brought on immense guilt so, I held the hurt inside. I was different and never felt like I belonged; this held me back, and my self-confidence suffered. My mother used to say, *Honey, hold your head up. You are beautiful, smart, and so loved. Why are you being so shy?* But this was much deeper than being shy. It was deep-rooted unworthiness and feeling like I was disconnected from everyone. My parents did not want to acknowledge the real me. So, if my perception that my biological father did not want me - which ironically became the truth - and my adoptive parents did not want to tell me anything about my adoption, I concluded that I must be damaged goods. For me, this translated into what is diagnosed as social anxiety today. I didn't speak out, being afraid my words would hurt someone. I believed that in order to be loved, I had to be perfect - and I knew I wasn't. I had so many thoughts running through my head, and I believed everyone could read my mind and my secret would come out; I would cause more pain for my Dad.

I felt I had to excel at everything, or no one would like me. Speaking up in a crowd was terrifying; in my mind, if I spoke up, others would think I was stupid. When I was criticized,

I shut down immediately. Being quiet came off as appearing shy or stuck up, of which I was neither. I probably came across this way because this was not my real authentic self that I kept hidden. I did try to fight my feelings. My mother and father were in denial, which led to a dead-end because I needed so desperately to hear the truth. It hurt me so much, and I had no support to cope or trust my feelings.

I had one man in my life who was my hero – my grandfather on my adoptive father's side. I never doubted Grandpa loved me unconditionally. He lived with Nanny on a farm not far from our house in a hamlet called Numogate. I watched wrestling with him – yup!! I was hooked. Every Saturday I spent there, I crawled up on his lap, and I remember him smelling like a mixture of pipe tobacco and Old Spice. We spent many summer mornings in the garden together, picking tomatoes and Golden Chief Corn. Golden Chief Corn was the best-tasting corn in the whole world. It may have been because we picked it together fresh off the stalks; I don't know, but I have never had better corn. We set up a roadside stand and sold the tomatoes, corn and other vegetables, bringing in what was left over for my Nanny to cook for supper along with her homemade bread. I loved watching my grandmother can fruit, make jam, and create beautiful quilts. She was very talented, and the quilts were designed and made to order for her customers. She made me a pink and white one with flowers and little Dutch girls. It was a true labour of love. There was a well on the farm, and in the morning, I drew the water by pumping it into jugs. I felt at home with Grandpa and Nanny, and I loved spending time on the farm. It was a simple life that I felt very peaceful in. They virtually lived off the land, which is a dying art.

In the winter, I went tobogganing down a hill near their farm. My best friend and I took our sleds and race down the hill at what we thought was lightning speed. It looked like a mountain to me, but it was really only a hill. Boy, those were such fun days; I felt so free. I loved being outdoors, growing up in Ontario, where there was always a lot of snow in the winter months. I built snow forts and snowmen and went on sleigh rides. I particularly enjoyed going into the woods on my father's snowmobile, where I could be alone with nature.

One particular night when I was around eight years old, I lay trying to sleep upstairs in my grandparents' guest room. There was a vicious thunderstorm, and I was frightened. They had company, and my Grandpa caught me sneaking down the stairs out of the corner of his eye, and he pointed to his lap. I crawled up onto its safety, and the lady who was visiting and I didn't know said, *Oh Bert, you are so good to her, especially since she's not your real granddaughter.* My hero set me down on the floor as he stood up from his rocking chair and firmly said, *How dare you! Get out of my house! She is mine! I don't want to see you again!* They left right away, and my Grandpa took me back up to my bed. Later, I found out the woman was his sister - I never saw her or her husband again. I was more confused than hurt as Grandpa tucked me in and told me that he and Nanny loved me very much. I never doubted that, and I never forgot that moment and how he made me feel so loved and secure. Grandpa fought for me and expressed loyalty to me in a way I had never experienced before. The next morning, Nanny spoke to me about what happened and told me not to worry about her. She said, *I never liked her anyway,* and we giggled about that.

I know my parents loved me, and I otherwise led a very privileged life. I don't blame them for any of what transpired. They feared if they spoke to me about my adoption, they would lose me, but that was the furthest thing from the truth.

Instead, they created wounds of fear and loneliness by ignoring my need to know who I came from. My parents could never acknowledge my pain because they simply did not have the tools, and I grasped tightly onto that pain as what was real to me. This transitioned into guilt, believing that if I allowed anyone to see inside the hurt little girl, I would in turn, hurt them. I did not want to see my father cry again at any cost.

Recently, I found a newspaper clipping that my mother gave me when I last saw her. It was a poem she had published in the local newspaper when I was around five years old. An anonymous author wrote it, and it greatly touched me.

> *Not of my flesh nor of my bone,*
> *but still miraculously my own.*
> *Never forget for a single minute*
> *You didn't grow under my heart but in it.*
> *God blessed me with a baby and*
> *now my baby is turning five.*
> *You are the light of my life and*
> *my reason to be alive.*
>
> *Love Mommy*

I was not aware of this public expression of love until I saw it at the age of 50. It melted my heart and continues to do so. If she had only been able to share this gift with me growing up, I feel it would have clarified so much for me.

I believe with all my heart that my adoptive parents meant well and that carrying this secret was not done with malice. They loved me the best way they could and knew how. I have forgiven them for not recognizing how disconnected I felt within the devastating childhood trauma of having my identity so far out of reach. They simply did not realize how much their decisions affected my self-confidence.

While vacuuming when I was 27 years old, a couple walked up to my front door one Friday afternoon. I remember thinking they must be coming to ask about our house as it was up for sale. My ex-husband answered the door and then told me to get changed because we had company, so I went upstairs and threw on some nicer clothes. When I came downstairs, I sat beside my husband on the couch. He didn't tell me he knew they were coming, but to this day, I believe he did. Throughout my life, I never went looking for my biological father because I knew that would hurt my parents.

The man sitting across from me asked, *Do you know who I am?* I had a feeling this person was in my home with news about my biological father, but I wasn't sure, so I asked if he was a lawyer. He answered that he was my father. At that moment, I hated everything about that man, and I said, *You can fuck off!* He rose to leave, but his wife, Valerie, told him to sit down. I started to cry, and he pulled out a picture of my natural mother and him at their wedding. I had no time to process this information and quickly pulled myself together, asking if anyone wanted a coffee. He abruptly told me they didn't drink coffee because they were practising Baptists. He shared that he found out where I lived from Myrtle Schneider, the lady from the church who gave me the carnation. At the time, I didn't know how she knew where I lived until he told me that the minister from the church and his wife were actually my grandparents. I learned a lot that day, including how ashamed he was of me and *how I turned out*. His words cut like a knife when he said, *If I had raised you, you would not have turned out this way.* My answer to him was, *Well, to be quite frank, you didn't raise me!* He got up abruptly, and his lovely wife said,

Paul, sit down. She was the head of the nursing school in Scarborough and a very strong lady. She asked if we would join them for dinner that evening at the hotel where they were staying. I reluctantly agreed. To this day, I do not know why I was confused and hurt, and I think I was in a bit of shock. He sent a limo around to the house with flowers, and it felt kind of odd - like he was trying to date me. When the waiter arrived at the table, my ex and I ordered a glass of wine. It was an awkward moment because, although my father said nothing at the time, I could tell he disapproved.

At the night's end, Paul asked if we would like to visit his home in Pickering, Ontario and meet my brother Alan. He also said he would arrange a party at a well-known hotel, The Omni King Edward, which was close by in Toronto, and I could meet my aunts and uncles and my biological grandmother. He told me that my grandfather had previously passed away. I told him I would call him later to set a date. After a few weeks, I called, and we put plans in motion to go to Pickering the following weekend. I was pregnant with four young children in tow when my ex and I headed out. We prepared the children for the journey of meeting a whole other side of their family. Part of me did not want to go because I think I was afraid of more rejection, but a part of me was curious about my newfound family.

This was to become one of the weirdest and saddest weekends of my life. After arriving late Friday evening and meeting my brother, Alan, I put the children to bed and then sat up with Valerie and my ex, talking for a bit. I noticed that Paul had disappeared and I thought this was strange, but I didn't know him all that well, and he mentioned earlier that he had work to do. Valerie discussed the following night's party with us and reassured me everyone was excited to meet me after all these years. I was nervous but also excited. To my amazement, Paul never came downstairs the next day. My ex and I took Alan and our children to McDonald's for lunch, and when we came back, Valerie informed us that the party was called off. There was no explanation given; confused, I looked at my ex-husband and asked if we should stay another night or go home? Although Alan was just a child, he asked us to please stay, and Valerie echoed the sentiment, so we decided to stay. Paul never came downstairs, and I never did get to meet the rest of my relatives, spending the night more confused than hurt. We left early the next morning after my father appeared and gave me a gold watch and my ex one hundred dollars. My watch stopped working a month later. Go figure. It felt like he gave me a retirement present, and in a funny way, I guess it was. To this day, my stomach goes in knots just thinking back on this bizarre weekend. I look back and think, *You have got to be flipping kidding me.* I never met my biological father again and was told he died many years later after suffering from Alzheimer's disease.

> ***There are many parents who give up children.***
> ***For most, the decision is made in the best interest of the child,***
> ***but my perception of why my natural father gave me up***
> ***was for selfish reasons.***

He told me that he wanted to continue pursuing his military career, so he had no choice but to give me up. There is a feeling of disrespect and unworthiness because I know he had other options but chose to give me away. From the time I met him, I associated my biological father's judgments on me and his selfishness with his religious belief system. Needless to say, I have been turned off of organized religion ever since.

The Beginning

I have a 48-year-old brother who is the same age as my oldest daughter, but I will never know him because I simply cannot open up that wound again. The weekend I met my father for the first time, my soul was ripped apart. I was forced to accept that he never wanted me as I sought validation through him, yet it was not to be. I have learned to reframe my quest to clarify *How dare he do this to me* to understanding that *it was never about me*. It has been a long journey over the years to reach the point of acceptance and move on from what transpired. I was angry afterwards, and it took a long time for me to process it all. I kicked and cried, moving through all levels of my pain. I talked out all the past shame and guilt with my friends until there were no more tears. I was able to reach a point of acceptance. Valerie asked for my help a few months later, telling me that Paul was in the hospital with a nervous breakdown. I had nothing more to give this man, and for my peace of mind, could not go down that road again. So, I chose to close that chapter and move on. A neighbour and I talked about this many years later, and Deanna said, *Ummm, that acorn fell really far from that tree, thank God!* We were able to laugh, both realizing that type of upbringing would have crushed my soul.

I wish I had the chance to sit down with him and explain how much his rejection hurt me. So, I sat at my dining room table alone yesterday and had a chat I thought I would have had with him. I thought this would be easy, but it was far from it. Feeling sad and weary of the baggage I had held onto for years, I told him that his explanation of giving me up was unfair and that he had other choices. I told him I was angry that he believed the choice he made was the only one he had. I went on to say that when he told me he gave me up to pursue his career, I felt abandoned all over again. I reiterated that I define love differently; real love is unconditional, and I found that with my adoptive parents. I also told him that his disapproval of how I grew up was not his to worry about. I grew up with parents who loved me. I also expressed gratitude for not having had to live a strict Christian life that followed judgemental religious principles, one within which he, not only once but twice, rejected the child he created. I shared how his deceit created a child's unworthiness that was carried into tear-filled painful nights for the rest of her life as she wondered if he was alive or dead and, if alive, why he wasn't with her. I wept again for the little girl who held on to secrets that once defined her. I wish I had the strength to tell him this when he hid in his room in Pickering, Ontario, all those years ago.

It took me years to become healthy enough to have that conversation with my biological father, and by then, he had passed away. I sat there at the table with my heart on my sleeve and my tea cooling. I felt the weight of his betrayal slowly lift off me - I was finally free. Internally I knew that forgiving him would unwrap my pain, and I could slowly move on. However, the little girl sometimes manages to creep back into my soul, but I have learned to slow down my thoughts, cry if I need to, and then let go.

The Beginning

Dorri, the Little Diva
Age three years
1956

III

Bringing up Dorri

I suspect my childhood was much like anyone else's - quite complicated and sometimes sad yet filled with happy and fun moments. I had a vivid imagination and was curious about other populations. Carrying my little girl's hurt inside of me, there were times when I felt overwhelmed, but I was also highly motivated by challenges and pushed on using humour to deflect my pain.

There were plenty of good times, mostly centered around my parent's cottage on Otter Lake or my best friend's family cottage on Rideau Lake. Water skiing was thrilling, and I was good at it, including slalom and doing jumps. I loved doing tricks on my skis while sailing over the water behind Dad's boat. I was happiest when pushing the boundaries and trying new skills. Being a bit of an entertainer on my skis, I always waved at people in other boats and onshore. My best friend, Nancy, and I often took the rowboat, and later my father's powerboat, across the bay, spending hours swimming. I remember going fishing with Dad, but it was the one and only time, and it did not last long. I got quite bored, and I was not a particularly quiet child, so he told me that fish don't bite when you are talking. My dad never took me fishing again.

The hallway at the elementary school I attended became quite familiar to me because I spent a lot of time there. I was the one who always got caught talking and, while I would never rat on my friends, I knew the teacher must have assumed

I was not talking to myself. I found it so unfair that I was singled out, and even though the extravert inside me wanted to use her voice, I was punished when I spoke out. So, after being criticized over and over again, I learned to shut down to protect myself. I remained talkative within my comfort zone, but if I ventured out of that bubble, I immediately clammed up. It was complicated, and so was I.

When I got in trouble for talking at school, my mother found out right away because she taught at the same school I attended. But when I was an adult within my career, I had the last laugh because I ended up conquering my fear of speaking up and put money where my mouth is. To this day, my youngest daughter tells me that I talk all the time when we are out. She says that I talk too much and to complete strangers. I guess one way of putting it is that I believe I am a natural storyteller, although she may have a different opinion. No matter what anyone thinks, I fed my children and put a roof over their heads using my voice, and as a result, I feel justified in doing so.

One of the more unfortunate occurrences in public school happened when I was in grade eight. My art teacher, Miss Barriger, held up one of my drawings during art class and said, *This is how not to do art*. I was humiliated beyond imagination. For many years, that statement created my belief that I could never be an artist and that I was somehow a disappointing failure. What a slap to my creativity!! From that day on, I questioned any artistic talent I might have. With plans to take a pottery class at the library that summer, I immediately decided not to attend because I feared my creations would be rejected. This feeling of inadequacy stayed with me until I visited the National Art Gallery in Ottawa when I was an adult. Looking up in front of me, I saw an art display of a two-by-four painted blue with a hydro transformer attached to one end. It was entitled *Life*. My lesson at that moment was clear .... *Art is an interpretation not a science.* Take that, Miss Barriger!!

When I was around nine or ten years old, I went to a summer camp with one of my friends. We arrived and assigned cabins. This place must have had the lowest budget going. My parents thought that because it was a church camp, it would be a good experience for me. We had oatmeal and toast each morning and bologna at dinner every night! Once again, I found myself thinking, *You have got to be kidding me! Really?* There were mosquitos in the cabin every night, and I could not sleep. I cried uncontrollably every night; I was incredibly homesick and just wanted to go home, which was an over two-hour drive away. By the third day they put me in the infirmary and called my mom, suggesting she come get me. She talked to me and told me to give the camp a chance. Abandonment reared its lonely head and placed my soul back into its confused state; I cried even harder. After another call from the camp, my mom came and picked me up.

> ***I wish I had the tools then that I have now to identify and overcome the trauma I experienced as a result of being away from my family and home, but I did not.***

The whole thing left me traumatized. Being that complicated child without an outlet to vent was frustrating, and it seemed that every time she needed to voice what she was going through, she was shut down. Once again, the hurt little girl inside of me felt unheard and unvalidated.

Those were the days when kids went outside to play after breakfast. My mom called me in for lunch, and then I went back out and didn't return until dark. My mother always called with a rather peculiar, almost operettic voice, which my friends thought was very funny. I remember being embarrassed and rushing home so she would stop. Now and then, Nancy and I rode our bicycles to the swamp to pick pussy willows or to a field to pick lilacs. We played with our dolls under the weeping willow tree in her backyard in her tent. We also spend hours selling lemonade at our roadside stand. My father built a rink in our backyard every winter for my friends and me to enjoy ice-skating on.

Travelling was a big part of my youth. We travelled abroad to England, Scotland, Wales, Ireland, and France. My father always chose bed and breakfast locations, and I remember sitting up late with him many nights, listening to the folklore of the places where we stayed. Learning about distant places and times fed my imagination as I felt empathy for the lives gone before me. I remember visiting my friend, Leslie, at her cottage for the first time; I met her through my mother's friend in England, and we became pen pals. Yes, way back in the day, we actually wrote letters by hand to people we met and sent them through the mail. Now, texting and messaging have taken over that beautiful tradition. That day, Leslie and I took her dog, *Duck*, for a walk through the Scottish Moors. We went back to our bed and breakfast, where a lady in a long black dress stood in the kitchen, stirring something in a huge pot on the stove - she gave my mom a jar of the jam she was making when we left. But at the time, I believed I had seen a witch. Having a very active imagination, I was frightened out of my mind and slept with one eye open all night.

We travelled to Scotland, stopping to see if we could get a glimpse of the Loch Ness Monster. I must have been taking too long trying to see it when my dad yelled, *There he is!* I shouted, *Where!!* My dad was quick to respond, *You just missed him. He will not be back again for a while.* He convinced me to hop back into the car, and we drove off. All this travelling provided me with a love of history. I was so happy exploring new places and meeting new people. Relationships are an important part of my life - listening to stories about people from different places and times allowed me to feel connected to them.

Paris held its own allure. The majesty of the cathedrals, the architecture of the ancient buildings, and the thrill of shopping in a place where fashion is iconic, won my heart. I was motivated to wake up every morning and write about my adventures in my diary. The language barrier did not seem so daunting as many spoke or understood English. I challenged myself to learn one new French word a day and practice it when we went out.

One summer, my parents and I travelled across Canada. We started out from the Ottawa, Ontario area, crossing Manitoba into the prairies. The prairies took a long time as one wheat field looked the same as the next one to this little girl. The saving grace was that this was the only time I was allowed to have as many Life Savers as I wanted. Looking back, I shake my head and laugh, knowing that was to keep me from talking too much.

I remember the beauty of the Rocky Mountains and the ski lift my parents and I went on in the hot springs in Banff, along with the horrible sulphur smell there. We continued on as far as Peachland in the Okanagan, ironically, where my husband, Drew, and I live now. We stopped there because my dad was running out of holiday time. We could have made the trip in less time and gone further, except my dad was living his lifelong fantasy of becoming an amateur photographer, stopping every few miles all the way to take a picture of something.

I also enjoyed a family trip to the east coast of Canada,

fulfilling every little girl's dream of seeing where Anne of Green Gables was created and visiting the series' author, Lucy Maud Montgomery's home in Prince Edward Island. The little girl in me has always identified with Anne. This area offered amazingly beautiful red sandy beaches, and I ate my first lobster on the shores of the Atlantic Ocean, a body of water that captivated me, even as a small child. I remember laying on my back in the red sand, thinking about this girl, Anne, from long ago. How she must have felt so free being surrounded by the wind coming off the ocean and the huge clouds drifting by. I longed to step back in time and become her, if only for a short time.

My parents loved to go to Florida every spring during March Break. We swam in the ocean and explored the cities we travelled through. Exploring fed my active imagination and formed an escape within my mind where I could belong. No one knew my secret in these make belief places, so I could confidently be me. Being a history buff, I loved discovering new communities and was happiest when we went on road trips.

When we weren't travelling, I remember writing plays performed in my backyard on the clothesline platform. I started by charging my friends a nickel to be in the play until my mother found out and made me give the money back. I guess my entrepreneurial spirit was a part of me even then, but maybe not in a good way. I enjoyed writing the plays and had fun while it lasted. I always dreamed of being a writer. This was the start of developing a skill set that proved to be hugely beneficial down the road. I enjoyed creating the story and directing the cast as well; this played into my love of being a leader. At such a young age, I recognized how important creativity was in my life, and even though I didn't identify this as a value at the time, I later discovered how authentic it was to me. Being able to trust my creative mind played out many years later, leading me into a career where I empathetically provided win-win scenarios for the clients I worked with.

In the fifties and sixties, most parents didn't have open and honest communication with their children about many things. My parents were not any different. If you ask my children, my parents were the greatest and the best grandparents, loving each and every one of them. And I would agree with them. What I have concluded is that it did not matter that I was adopted. I indeed had two parents who loved me, and I was a privileged child in so many ways. Unfortunately, it was the secrecy and white lies that sought to define my reality, which was what tormented my heart. My parents loved me; of that, I have no doubt. But my confusion and guilt stood in the way of me becoming my true self. The real me, the creative, outgoing person that I was going to become, was yet to be recognized, especially by me.

This was such a heavy burden for my young self to bare. Holding me accountable for the secrets held by adults was destructive.

Even though my mother loved me so much, she denied sharing the facts of my birth and adoption with me. I carried the weight of the guilt associated with my birth, and along with that came a huge disconnect from those around me. I sought validation from the very people who could not or would not give it to me. I loved my adoptive parents, and I know they loved me. However, that guilt and disconnection persisted well into the future. I was not taught how to process feelings, so I pushed them down until I could deny them. This was not emotionally healthy, and in fact, created more guilt - of what I was not sure, but guilty just the same. I was encouraged to recognize emotions as a weakness. If I was sad, they would fix it. If I was happy, I was being silly. My parents did not allow me to fail. I suppose they felt they were protecting me; I simultaneously learned how not to cope with failure or how to problem-solve. This co-dependency made me believe I could not do anything without help – I learned to let that belief go many years ago and placed boundaries around those who enabled it.

I do not blame my mother for how differently we communicated our love. She did so by making certain I had all the gifts any little girl could ever want. To me, love meant verbally sharing each other's emotions, and she had a difficult time doing this. To this day, I am not one hundred percent certain why she was averse to expressing how she felt or telling me where and who I came from. All I know is that we had this disconnect in communication; we just did. When I reflect on this, I think we were both overwhelmed when it came to speaking about my adoption. I was overwhelmed with fear of hurting her or my dad, and perhaps she felt safer not mentioning it. I remember moments when I thought my youngest aunt was on the verge of telling me more about her sister, but out of respect for my mother, she held back.

I have been so afraid to go back to those mixed-up, complicated days that I put myself in a bubble. There are many people from back in the day who meant the world to me, yet I had to let some go in order to protect me from the haunting memories of my past. Lately, I reached out to a few through social media; I never meant to hurt them, even though I know I did by creating years of distance. The past when I was so bruised is still a mountain I am working on climbing. There are times when it terrifies me, yet I know, whatever the end result, I am not that little girl in hiding anymore, and I want to share my story of why I rejected them. I still have work to do because that is not clear to me yet.

It would take a massive shake-up in my life to completely lift those self-sabotaging thoughts and overcome the powerlessness I accepted as my norm so long ago. How I overcame the challenges to the degree I have, forms my story. I learned later in life that the validation I sought doesn't come from others but instead from within me. That validation is what honours my truth, my unique self. As I moved forward, I somehow overcame the social anxiety that debilitated me in my childhood. I needed to get beyond that place to truly heal. Life threw me some major storms, and how I chose to venture out of them is how I redefined my perceptions and intentions, overcoming my trauma. I visualized that my challenges could be overcome, and I was able to move forward leaving the past where it belongs ... in the past. This allowed me the wisdom to reflect back and make changes moving forward.

I do not believe that I lost myself.
I simply reclaimed who I was despite
being conditioned to be different.
My soul was in there waiting to be discovered,
and when my soul became my truth,
it was a joyful thing.

High school does not hold many fond memories as I struggled even though or because my grades were better than average. I completed four grades in two years and ended up graduating with my Grade 13 diploma at the age of 15. Just like in elementary school, I tried to fit in; I was an awkward child, to say at the least. I went out on a date with a local boy who played hockey. When he arrived at my house, I could smell alcohol on his breath, but I didn't think he was intoxicated. We went off to a dance in town at Hanley Hall, taking a shortcut through a subway tunnel. Approaching the front of the tunnel, Kenny pushed me up against a wall and started to pull off my blouse. This scared the shit out of me, and I kneed him in the groin. I ran like hell and arrived at the hall in a matter of minutes. Lucky for me, a boy who I had previously dated saw me. Dave ran over to me and asked, *Who did this to you?* I was crying hard at this point, so he gently grabbed my arm and took me to his car. I told him what happened, and he told me that his parents were out curling, so I could go back to his place to get cleaned up before taking me home. I got cleaned up, and we ordered a pizza. After we ate, he took me home. I look back on that day as a true experience of both evil and good. The next day Kenny's sister and one of his friends called me, begging me not to tell anyone what had happened as Kenny was up for a scholarship to play hockey in the United States. I said I wouldn't, but I never got an apology from him. He just wanted to save his own skin. I was only 14 years old at the time, and being naïve, I don't think I recognized the seriousness of what happened to me. I never told my parents because I thought I might get in trouble - for what, I do not know. It all makes sense now, knowing that I was afraid they would be hurt, and I was a people pleaser after all. I also know that Kenny wanted to hurt me, and I am proud that I sensed that danger and intuitively knew how to protect myself by hurting him and running away.

Years later, I look back with hope that he didn't try it on any other young girl. I had not thought about it for a long time until 2018 when I was watching the news, and Brett Kavanagh, who was being nominated to serve on the United States Supreme

Court, was being accused of sexual assault. It is said that they did not believe his accuser because she was fuzzy on the date the alleged assault occurred. I, too, do not remember the exact date that Kenny violated me, but I clearly recall every detail of what he did to me. It is so difficult for young girls, women, men, and people of all genders to find the courage to report rape, sexual assault, or attempted rape because, even today, the system cannot be trusted, often revictimizing the very person who has gone through the trauma.

My childhood friends were still in elementary school and two grades behind me when I entered high school, and besides our age difference, I didn't have a lot in common with my classmates. There was the expectation for me to behave older than I was, but I was still treated like a little girl at home. This was confusing as I did not know where I belonged. My classmates went to parties and dances, and my parents felt I was too young to join them - and I probably was. Once again, it was complicated. I was too young for the boys my peers were dating, and boys my age seemed too young for me, ending up being my friends who often came to me for dating advice. I, therefore, dated boys from out of town. To me, it was just another piece of the disconnection I struggled with. I was lonely except when I played sports. I played basketball, was on the cheerleading squad and the gymnastic team. Sports gave me the happiness and connection I craved with my peers. I was good at the uneven bars, did well on the basketball court, and loved being a cheerleader, so others accepted me on these teams. I also used sports as an outlet for my voice - in my high school yearbook, I was deemed the person anyone could go to for support on any matter of things. I did not recognize that this was how my peers perceived me. It was a true honour.

I held a summer job at the Rideau Regional Hospital

during the summer of 1970. I was in charge of developing a nursery school program for those who the hospital deemed educatable children. Another girl, Cheryl, and I were in charge of developing a pilot project designed to help institutionalized children between the ages of eight and ten years identify colors, count to ten, and develop higher levels of interpersonal communication skills. We were also asked to create opportunities for these children for better social interaction. I had no formal training in developing such a program, but I did have a real desire to make a difference in the lives of these kids. We designed the program, and the staff on the wards chose the children they thought would be a good fit. It was awe-inspiring to see the personal growth these young children achieved in just two and a half months. Previous to this program, the children seldom left their wards. They ate, played, and slept in a ward with no stimulation for growth. Most of my little children under my supervision were born with down syndrome or autism. *They called me Mommy*, and that was ok. The pride on their faces and the joy they experienced while achieving simple tasks was a blessing for us all. One of my favourite memories was of a young boy diagnosed with low spectrum autism who achieved the ability to blow out a match. Eddie came out of his self-enclosed bubble, proudly reacting to this seemingly small task by clapping his hands in elation. I will never forget the wide grin on his face when every one of his classmates clapped along - little ones are so eager to please. It may not have sounded like a big deal to the outside world, but it meant everything to these children. This nursery school was held from June to September that year. Sadly, I believe the program was discontinued.

    I used to go back to the hospital on Saturdays and take Johnny, a little eight-year-old with Down syndrome, out of his ward to see the town. He got so excited watching the traffic lights change colours. We went to eat at a Chinese food restaurant that he loved. My co-worker, Cheryl, came with me, bringing Eddie, the little boy who had autism. It was such a happy time with these little guys. Sometimes, we went to the library and read a book to them. Johnny loved the puzzles, but Eddie was often frustrated. My favourite place to go with these guys was the playground. We needed to teach them how to use the slides and swings - they were leery at first, but they got the hang of it the more we went. They had the chance to run around and enjoy the simple pleasures that delighted and amazed these little guys, the ones that most children take for granted. It was humbling to see them expand their horizons.

I remember feeling so grateful to receive an opportunity to help and encourage children who needed stimulation. Taking ownership of my accomplishment, I found pride within me for the first time. And as much as this felt incredible, I was also sad that my parents could not recognize the great work I was doing and how it positively affected the lives of the wee guys in the program. This was the first time I identified what was truly important to me; it fed my creative side, whereby I was given the freedom to write the program and implement it using empathy and respect to guide me. I had hoped that my parents would be proud of me, but that was not evident to me. My accomplishments went unnoticed, other than the odd, *Oh that's nice dear*, we never discussed the work I did – it's like it didn't matter.

Dorri's first set of wheels

IV

Turning Storms Into Rainbows

I wasn't an angel by any means, but I wasn't considered a rebel like most teenagers in my age group. In 1970, I met my now ex-husband. We dated, and I fell in love and became pregnant with our first child. I was young, but that did not deter me from having my baby; I cherished her from day one. We were married in a small country church just before the birth of my daughter. I believed that I finally found what made me whole. I was a wife and mother of a precious baby girl, and every time I looked at her, a wave of calm enveloped me. I loved my family, and I was happy. This was the life I always hoped for. From there, we had seven more children.

For all intents and purposes, we looked like a loving family. No one could tell we were anything but happy from the outside. My ex and I, our friends, and his family went on many adventures to the ski hills: Mont Tremblant, Lake Placid, Mont Saint Anne, and eventually, Whistler. I wasn't a tremendously talented skier, but I tried hard and had tons of fun. One winter, we won a family ski pass to Mount Tremblant. It was interesting that they looked surprised at our family of six when we went to claim our prize, telling us the prize was for immediate family only. After stating, *Yes, indeed, that is exactly what we are*, they reluctantly wrote out the passes. Not long after, they put a limit on the number of family members per prize.

My ex loved Christmas, and he cooked dinner every

Christmas Eve. One year, he tried to introduce us to moose meat. I could not believe it!! Other years, we ordered Chinese food or pizza. He also delighted in playing Santa, and our children always crept down the stairs after he lit the fireplace and plugged in the tree lights. It was a role he appeared to revel in. Every year, our three older girls practiced a play I had written, and they performed it for him on Christmas Eve; the girls had so much fun. I loved writing plays throughout those years, and I felt truly happy and believed that I was loved. He was the only one who could do the turkey because I had never learned how to cook, and he loved to. When I went to a lawyer years later, she asked me what I wanted from the divorce. I told her that all I wanted was a Costco card and a cooked turkey every Christmas. She tried not to laugh, telling me she could get me a Costco card but probably not the turkey.

Bringing up my amazing *crazy eights* was never boring. My eldest loved figure skating and excelled at it, while my second daughter said, *My feet get cold; I don't like it*. When my second little girl went to school, there was always some sort of drama. I got a call one afternoon from the principal of the elementary school my girls attended. He said, *Mrs. Jones, your daughter is on the floor and will not get up*. I replied, Really? Since the school was directly across from our house, he asked me to come and see if I could talk to her; I agreed. When I arrived, there she was on a tipped-over chair on the floor. I looked at her and said, *Sweetie, what are you doing?* She told me that the teacher told her to get up off the floor, and my daughter told her, I cannot not do that. Puzzled, I asked her, *Why not*. Her answer was *Because I am on the chair, not the floor*. There never was a dull moment with that little girl!!

We enjoyed spending time at my parent's cottage on Otter Lake in Ontario. The children loved to swim and have picnics with their nanny and me. We had bonfires when the weather permitted. The chipmunks were so tame they used to take food right out of our hands. There was no indoor plumbing and no telephone service because my father wanted a place where he could get back to the art of living off the land as he had on my grandparent's farm. We brought in drinking water from the nearby town, but I hauled water from the lake to boil for bathing and cooking. Although I didn't mind pumping the water manually, my father eventually hooked up a pump system to the sink. We used an outhouse, and the neighbours commented they could tell when Dorri arrived for the summer as I disinfected the interior and used so much bathroom spray that the smell wafted over to their cottages. There was no television because the outdoor life was enough. On rainy days, the children and I read, played cards and did crafts. When my mother drove up to the lake, we sometimes went out for lunch and would return to her house to get showered and buy groceries. Looking back now, I realize how much I miss the simple pleasures this type of rustic living provided. I was always in my happy place when at the lake.

Life seemed to be going well until a plot twist developed. To my dismay, five years into our marriage, it suffered a blow when I found out he had his first of many affairs. I always accepted his indiscretions as my fault. They left me believing I was not enough for him to love. This seemed to be a reoccurring theme in my life, bringing back the feelings of unworthiness I suffered as a child; I was back there again. Many years later, I became aware that being caught in an abusive relationship was not about me. But that was not something I believed at the time. I learned that lesson the hard way, always taking him back after he apologized. I had this self-defeating thought that being with a cheater was better than being alone. When I was really sad, my daughter would point her finger and say,

Mommy, it isn't about you;
it's about him.

I recognize now that I did not deserve to be treated that way and none of it had anything to do with me. But back then, I tried to change everything about myself. I even moved with him from Ontario to British Columbia so he could pursue a business opportunity with his brother. The children and I waited back in Ontario for him to send for us. He told us it would only be a couple of weeks until he found us a house to rent. The weeks turn into a month and then six weeks. It was embarrassing and very hurtful. My heart could not face the reality of what my head knew. I was homeless and couch-surfing with our six children while eight months pregnant with our seventh child. I felt unwanted and unloved. However, he kept telling me to be patient, telling me it wouldn't be much longer as he continued looking for our home.

Eventually, my mother paid for our one-way tickets to Vancouver, afraid the stress would cause me to lose our baby I was carrying. But all that did was take me away from my family and friends in Ontario, and it didn't really work out very well. I viewed this move as a new chance for us, a chance to start over again. Apparently, I did not receive the right memo as he left our eight children and me five years after we moved to Vancouver after being married for a little over twenty years. Our marriage literally took the last bit of my self-esteem. I guess I was a slow learner. *I could have, should have,* would have left years before, but my need to fix my marriage and keep my family together was so very strong. Denial kept me from committing to the changes I needed to take to move on. The little hurt girl inside me kept saying, *You cannot do this alone.* This perception led me to extremely low self-esteem and lack of self-confidence.

There were many times I thought about taking the children and leaving - but to where and with what money? I knew my parents would take us in, but I also instinctively knew that I could not survive living with them, being that little girl again. So, I stayed and hoped he would see the love I held for him and come home to his family. I attached myself so deeply to the idea of being his wife that the thought of me existing without him terrified me. After all, he was my best friend, wasn't he? There are many times I look back and wonder what the heck was I thinking.

My perception was that I was in a loving marriage. But I own that misperception because it did not exist. I always tried to change everything I could to please him, and although there were times when I felt angry, I rarely acknowledged it. I internalized it until that anger became guilt and then self-blame. I am a true people-pleaser who, at my worst, accepted the blame he deflected on me. The egoic control I felt he had over me created my motivation to constantly try being worthy of his love. I worked with a fever at being prettier and thinner, along with being a better wife, mother, and human. It was a battle I never won.

My ex told untruths about me after he left that made me feel unbelievably unloved and disrespected. I have finally put those words in the past, no longer having any power over me. I have compassion for him now as I believe his lies were to justify his actions to others. It makes me sad to think he needed to do that. Even then, I was not angry; I was simply hurt. I believe the biggest challenge was dealing with many different age groups and personalities that made up my family. I was the one parent they had, and I was falling apart. Each age group had different reactions and responses to the separation, and it was difficult for me to be entirely present and in the moment for everyone at the same time. It was totally my responsibility to keep them healthy in every way, and I was emotionally drained. I still intended to keep my children safe with the knowledge that their mother loved them unconditionally.

The only time my anger surfaced was when I saw how his leaving hurt my children. I saw first-hand that when a parent appears to stop loving their child, the child does not hate the parent but instead hates themself. I saw the anger and the hurt they were experiencing, but I could not fix their guilt and self-blame. To this day, it pains me that I could not alleviate their shame, even though I could not undo what he did. That was and still is up to him.

When my ex-husband left, I went stir crazy. Grief took over as if he had died, and in some ways, he had to me. But, with an empty bank account, I had no time to grieve him. I had to think of my eight children and make a plan to move on. At first, I took to drinking more than I should and cried many, many nights. However, my pity party was short-lived with mouths to feed, children to clothe, and all of us suffering. So, I put on my big girl panties and forged ahead into the unknown. I often wonder how I did it, and I have come to the awareness that I survived because I finally realized that my children's father mistreated me because he had his own internal battles that had nothing to do with me.

> ***I then found the grace to forgive,***
> ***knowing that revenge had no place***
> ***within my intentions.***

Those times were not easy. I remember feeling very sad and terribly alone one day. A friend of mine called me and heard me crying through my words as I share how overwhelmed I was.

Kim told me to look out my window and asked me what I saw. I looked and saw my youngest son on his rollerblades, taking shots at his hockey net. I listened intently to her response, telling me that my ex was not worthy of my tears but that I had this incredible chance to love my children through these dark days and to be loved back by those same children until my days got better. I will never forget her words, *You are all they have!* She was right, and they are all I will ever want. My ex-husband told me how sorry he was years later at my son's funeral. I had nothing to say but, *Thank you.* He now has a relationship, albeit complicated, with our children. They totally understand what unconditional love is and that it does not mean accepting bad behaviour but loving someone despite it – they have shown me that. I must admit that it sometimes still stings. However, I remind myself that he is their father and they are adults; there need not be competition between us. I have no doubt at all that Drew and I reside in a huge place in their hearts. In a strange way, his leaving opened a whole new world of possibilities in which I found my strength. Maybe I should thank him, but I am not ready for that just yet; I will leave that for another day.

My children came in a full range of ages. When we moved into a new house, inevitably, a mother would come over and ask if I had a child the same age as one of their sons or daughters. I immediately said yes without them telling me their child's age – I simply knew we had one.

When my ex left, my children ranged from late teens to the youngest being just four years old. Ideally, I would have liked both my children's father and I involved in supporting them physically, emotionally, and financially. But this was not to be the case. It was extremely difficult when their whole world became uprooted, and I was utterly overwhelmed. If I could do it over again, I would do many things differently, having had more age-appropriate conversations with my kids and taking the time to notice their wounds more readily. But we were all in survival mode, and somehow, someway, we got through those days.

My ex was a trigger for me, so there were times I let them know I blamed him - I could have listened more and shared less. However, those days are long gone, and I cannot go back and have a redo. As one person told me, my conversations with them were filled with good intentions but not always perceived as such. My goal was always to keep us alive and to keep our family on the side of love - which I did. I learned to turn hurt into hope to heal, and more often than not, that hope was all I needed to move forward. For me, through all the twists and turns, blind faith, along with good intentions and purpose, got us to the other side.

Time was fleeting for me. I learned to live with the thought that I was losing my marbles, and there were times I believed that. The pain was devastating and letting go of the anxiety that held this little girl hostage for so long became imperative to my mental health. Choosing to tell her, *Not Today, I have work to do*, allowed me to dismiss her and put any thoughts that I might fail on the back burner so that I could forge ahead.

> ***I have learned to embrace that little girl***
> ***Because she also serves as a warning***
> ***to slow my reactions down***
> ***and think about how I want to respond.***

I had to find that courage to move forward. What I didn't realize was that I was actually enough for him, but I didn't believe I was enough for me. Somehow, somewhere, I had lost my authentic self, and it was time to become me again. I never intended to become a victim, but rather, always defined myself as a survivor. I spent 20 years trying to please a man whose issues were not mine to fix, and once I realized I had given the one person who caused me pain all my power, I discovered it was only me who could take my power back. And take it back, I did!!

I had to adapt to a newfound reality overnight, and I had to go through that storm alone. I was deeply saddened and, once again, felt disconnected from the world that became my normal - even and especially if that normal was dysfunctional and disempowering. It was time I found the strength within to reclaim connection again. I had no idea how to do that. I remember thinking of how deserted I felt as a child and how my own children were experiencing the same, facing their father's abandonment. I managed two layers to all of this - the pain I felt personally and the pain my children experienced. I was determined that I would be the parent who would help ease the pain. I knew I was far from perfect, but I vowed I would do my best. And if I'm sure of anything, it is that I gave my children my best. Did I make mistakes? Of course, I did, but I never once gave up on my family. I stopped giving energy to what was in the past and focused on building anew. Was letting go easy? Not one little bit. However, I did not have the time or finances to delve into the *what-ifs*. I focused my reality on my family and what became our journey to heal with my intention to care for them and take our situation from a place of loss to one of success for everyone. Our family unit looked different as it was fractured, yet I vowed I would make it whole one day.

Despite all the struggles my children and I went through, I believe the love and respect we had for one another was the glue that held us together. My oldest daughter supported me to overcome many obstacles and encouraged me to continue fighting to find my strength. My second oldest daughter also helped by doing things like buying my youngest a pair of basketball shoes that I could not afford. She was putting herself through university at the time and was waitressing to make ends meet. These were kind and generous acts that I am so grateful for. We managed to build a caring foundation that supported all of us to move forward. Their incredible love carries on to this day and is mirrored in this quote I read just the other day:

Strength is what we gain from the madness we survive.

And indeed, we did.

It took a while to recognize that I could, indeed, survive. What an eye-opener - I call this my *aha* moment. This didn't occur as an insight all at once. It became a journey to self-discovery, and what I realized was that while going through the eye of the storm I wasn't so sure I could make it out, but I did. Nor did I go through a storm of this magnitude without being forever changed. I have seldom gone through any storm and stayed the same. They say that time heals all wounds, but I do not believe that to be true. I believe that by using perception and intention, I could move forward. I define this belief in this way:

Perception comes from a place where I believe in myself and the possibility I could make things happen. Intention becomes an instrument for change .

It was always my intention to make it through those hard

times. I just didn't know how, but deep inside me, I always knew I could.

My journey with this perception and intention began healing the scars left behind. I had no idea what to do; after all, I was a newly single stay-at-home mother, and I recognized that this would not pay the bills. Raising eight children on my own was difficult, but there was no question I was staying rather than stepping away. They already lost one parent - they simply could not lose another. My children were and are my world. I wasn't a perfect parent because I am not a perfect human being. I did all I knew the best way I could to provide for my sweet children in all aspects of their lives. I think what saved us was taking turns going wham bat crazy ... luckily, not all on the same day. And we all had our roles. My children are my heroes.

We weathered the storm together, grew stronger, and did not give up. To this day, they are my best friends, and I know how much love they share as siblings. When the chips are down, they have each other's back, even when issues arise between them; they are siblings after all. But every holiday or birthday sees them gather, albeit before Covid! My oldest daughter helped me so much during these days; she was a true champion, holding all our hands through every bit of insanity. I have eight awesome children and three wonderful grandchildren, and I am constantly rewarded by their love and support. My relationship with each of them may look different from the outside, but they all know I would not trade our love for anything. In fact, I used to take each one of them aside and tell them they were my favourite child and why. They soon caught on and laugh about it to this day.

While my children were growing up, I tried my best to spend individual time with each of them. Sometimes, I kept my one daughter home from school to watch *I Love Lucy* together.

My youngest daughter and I had a standing date to shop at Costco every Saturday morning. And my third girl remembers when I took her out of school to go to the mall for lunch. She told me recently that she fondly remembers the day we picked out one of her Halloween costumes. It seemed like such a small thing at the time, but as one of eight children, it meant a lot to them to have that one-on-one attention. I was the loudest, proudest fan at their sports games, and my one daughter had the humiliating experience of me yelling at the referee at her basketball game. I decided he was calling too many penalties, and I shouted out, *If I had known this was a sleepover, I would have worn my pyjamas.* When she went to take a free shot, the referee asked her if I was her mother. She sheepishly admitted I was, and he just laughed. I was passionate about supporting my children, and there were times I could have toned it down just a snitch - not every child's mother has been red-carded at her son's soccer game!! I proudly hold that distinct honour, although my son might disagree with the honour part. I come honestly by the trait of being passionate. I remember playing Aunt Polly in my high school production of Tom Sawyer with my mother sitting in the auditorium. When I came on stage, she stood up and shouted, *Honey, we are over here.* Both my mother and I had great intentions; however, the executions may have left a little to be desired.

My parents lived 4000 miles away, and when my husband left, I felt overwhelmed and very afraid. My father had just suffered a stroke, so this was not a time to reach out to them. I was venturing into a whole other world, one of huge responsibility fraught with challenges - one I was not prepared for. I felt broken and torn into pieces, crying an ocean full of tears of sadness, loneliness, and fear. Desperation set in as, needless to say, my world changed in an instant and forever.

I never expected my ex to be emotionally supportive, but he also did not provide for his children financially. I consistently tried to have him pay child support, but he always seemed to slip through the cracks. In fact, I became so overwhelmed one day that I tried to run away. I had a particularly stressful day, and I just wanted to get in the car and drive - to where I did not know or did not care...just away. Just as I was getting in the car, my daughter came out and asked, *Where you are going, Mom*. I answered, *I'm running away*. She looked at me and said, *I am coming with you*. Without hesitating, I told her to get in the car. One by one, several more of my children came out and got in the car, and I realized I was taking the exact people I thought I needed space from with me. I drove back up the driveway, stopped the car, got out and ran for my bedroom, telling them that unless there was a flipping fire, DO NOT bug me for the next hour. It worked...for an hour.

I learned a lot while single parenting this brilliant bunch of coconuts. In hindsight, I discovered that effective communication skills are imperative to parenting successfully and that staying in tune with each of my children earned their trust while refraining from judging their emotions – I learned from my experience with my parents that a child's feelings are valid even when not understanding them. Questions become useful when not being afraid to answer openly and honestly. I placed value on what they were going through and assisted them to problem-solve to the best of my ability. I now know that instead of fixing their problems, it's best to provide them with the tools they need to fix them independently. Beginning early on in their lives, I developed clear but fair boundaries. When they were young, my oldest daughter felt like a friend because I was so young when I had her and didn't know how to be a parent. With each additional child and the experience that came with them, I took on more of an adult role while supporting them through their ups and downs rather than being their friend.

I believe in respecting children's individual paths and trusting that, at the end of the day, they will acquire the coping skills to live life with purpose. My hope is that my children recognize how unique each is in this world. I do not beat myself up for having to learn much of this in hindsight. If I had known better, I would have done better. I do this without apology as the love I felt for every one of them was and is genuine. This is the reason I fought so hard - always to give them everything within me. I found that the younger children asked questions that required honest but short answers, while the older ones were confused and needed more clarity. My children's world was rocked, and I knew they would be best served by not allowing them to self-blame. They were as overwhelmed and hurt as I was. My one daughter told me that she remembers when her father left; she was so relieved the fighting had stopped, but my tears at night made her wonder if she was naive. It was a confusing time for all of us, with each processing the pain in different ways.

Turning Storms Into Rainbows

This is a shot taken off my deck across the lake from
Okanagan Mountain.
Life saw me tackle several storms.
They were all significant in their ability to turn
themselves into rainbows.
Within this perception,
I discovered the intention of making what I want happen,
and the skies always magically become beautiful again.

V

Getting My Ducks In A Row

I adore and treasure the connection I have with my children. Throughout everything we have gone through, I cherish the funs times we always managed to have. When they were younger, we went camping every summer; not all that successfully, but we went year after year anyway. Our favourite spot was Golden Ears Park, where reservations had to be made ahead of time and could not be refunded. I didn't have any money to waste, so we went regardless of the weather, rain or cold. Because I never camped before in my life, the boys attempted to put up our tents, and they did a pretty good job. My one daughter's boyfriend, who is now my son-in-law, came with us the first few times we went, and he taught the boys how to set up camp. We started our campfires with a Safeway log.

Not being prepared for the ton of money these adventures usually cost me, we didn't have any tarps, so when it rained, it meant going into town for all our meals, and that added up. Someone's air mattress always managed to get a hole in it, which meant another trip into town to buy a new one. However, on sunny days, we did enjoy ourselves swimming, renting pedal boats, and having pirate boat chases. One time, we even rented horses, and I didn't think I would ever walk again. The children often brought friends with them, and that was fine with me. Why not take everyone on an adventure in the woods whereby the one adult in charge was totally inexperienced? This could have been a recipe for disaster, but even if I didn't have all my marbles, we made it happen. Hot chocolate with Baileys at night around the campfire was delightful. My son was concerned about the wildlife, so, as his mother, I decided to show him that there was nothing to be afraid of. We went off on a hiking trail, just my son and me. Everything was going very well until we heard a huge howling noise in the bush. I calmed him down, saying it's probably just someone's dog. As we went further, the park ranger caught up with us and told us we had to immediately leave because there were a mother coyote and her cub in the vicinity. We both scooted out of there as fast as we could. This was to be my one and only act as a nature guide.

On another one of our misadventures, we went camping at Lac la Hach. It was in a private campground right on the lake, and one of my friends rented one of the cabins on the property, and we set up tents outside the cabin. We enjoyed tubing behind his boat, as well as making bonfires and listening to the sound of the loons late at night on the small but peaceful lake. One night as we lay in our tents sleeping, we were awakened by a strange roar followed by a huge splash. My children were as frightened as I was, but I warned them to stay in their tents and be very quiet. No one slept that night. Come daybreak, the campground owner came over to my tent and told me it was a mountain lion that broke the silence during the night. He assumed that, because she had gone into the lake, she must have been sick. We did not go camping again.

The memory of looking for a puppy to buy with my youngest daughter still warms my heart. We started at the SPCA, Society for the Prevention of Cruelty to Animals, but all they had at that time were Mastiffs and German Shepherds, and I wanted a chocolate Lab. We went to Pet Smart and another pet store in the mall to no avail, and the last place we looked was in a shop I really didn't want to buy from as it had a reputation of getting their dogs from a puppy mill. However, when we went into the store, we looked in the cages, and there was a pug. This little guy was so cute, so I asked to see him. My daughter and I fell in love with his face immediately. We also asked to see a Maltese, and when we had them both out at the same time, the pug kept pushing the other pup out of the way. When you know, you know! So, home we went with our adorable puppy, who we named Charlie. I brought him in, and my son said, *I thought you were getting a chocolate Lab? What did you do, shrink him?* He became a part of our family very quickly. Another one of my sons loved to walk him. He called him Charles and said he was a chick magnet. When Drew met him, he asked, *What the heck is that?!* I answered, *Our pug!* He looked confused as to what he was looking at, but we took him home anyway. Amazingly enough, Drew had never seen a pug before. He used to call him dumb as a stick in the same tone someone would say *I love you.*

From day one, Charlie had a special place in our hearts. As any pug owner will tell you, they are quite the characters; stubborn, loyal, and silly at times. He never ran in a straight line but instead had a hopping way of moving around. When he got old, my daughter called him Smelly Dog - like Smelly Cat on the show Friends - because he smelled horrible even though he was groomed regularly. He was my constant companion and passed away at the age of 15. I held him in my arms as he slipped away. I told him to go to my son, Nicky, who was waiting, and he took his last breath. His loss was enormous for all of us - when I went into the bedroom to tell Drew, he began sobbing. He asked me who he would call *dumb as a stick*; I volunteered.

Being my children's mother is my passion. They were, and

are still to this day, my entire world. Memories continuously flow of trips to our neighbourhood park. I remember taking the oldest five to the park, and one day, someone asked me if I had a daycare. I have to admit that hearing a comment like this brought out the sarcastic mamma bear bitch in me. My answer was *no, but if you find their parents, let me know*. Another time, someone asked me where my five children came from. *Mars*, I answered. I considered these questions disrespectful and found people so interesting. I wondered what they would say if I told them that I went on to find three more in the cabbage patch!

One afternoon, I heard a knock on the door and when I answered it, in barged two women who announced they were from the Children's Aid Society. As we spoke, one was looking behind my couch and curtains, and I asked what all this was about. She told me they had a complaint that I was running an illegal daycare. I started laughing and explained that all five children I had in my home were my own. They left shortly afterwards, explaining they were sorry, but they had to investigate all complaints legally. The next day, my son's teacher called me, wondering if I was ill. I said, *No, why?* She said, *Your son told me his mother has aids*. After I choked back a laugh, I explained what had happened. I don't know if she was embarrassed or not, but I found the conversation to be a little odd and quite funny at the same time.

Life with my children was never dull. In fact, we had incredibly exciting moments. For example, one evening, while sitting in my living room relaxing after work, I saw police cars with their lights on outside my door. I did not have time to question what they were doing there because as soon as I noticed them, there was a huge bang at my door. I opened it to three police officers facing me with guns drawn. They rushed past me and ran upstairs. I was shaking when one of the officers came back to inform me that, *You are being robbed as we speak.* I was speechless. I had not seen my boys since I got home, but I wasn't worried about them because I assumed they were out playing road hockey as it wasn't late, and that's what they often did. When the police searched my backyard, they came upon one of my sons hiding in the bushes. An officer brought him to me and asked if this was indeed my son. I replied, *Yes, why?* Well, apparently, a passerby saw three boys climbing out of our bathroom window onto our roof, and he called the police. It turns out the culprits were my boys, playing cops and robbers. One of the officers gave them all a lecture about the dangers of climbing onto and jumping off a roof, while another officer winked at me over their heads.

We had another encounter with the RCMP one evening after my daughter had just returned home after a date. I woke up after hearing suspicious noises that sounded like footsteps outside; I checked all the bedrooms to see if the children were asleep, and they were. I ruled out any of them being the cause, and then my daughter came out to me, saying she heard it as well. Since we both confirmed hearing something, I thought it was a good idea to phone 9-1-1. We did not see the police car arrive and continued to wait. All of a sudden, we heard footsteps coming up the back stairs that led to a deck. My daughter grabbed a frying pan, ready and willing to attack. A loud voice yelled, *Please don't hurt me!* This is the police. In came a constable, and interestingly, the first thing I noticed was how cute he was. He immediately assured us they could not find anything and suggested it might have been raccoons. Okay, that was our evening of excitement.

Just the other day, my son reminded me about New Year's Eve in 1999. We all dressed up and went out for dinner at a five-star restaurant, *Seasons on the Park*. It was expensive, but I had saved up for it, and after all, it was a special night as we were entering into a new millennium. I wanted my children to experience this celebration and make lasting memories moving into 2000. After our meal, we headed home, where I had invited several friends to join us for nibbles and drinks. We put on music, and some people were dancing when the clock struck midnight. My daughter ran outside with a pot and started banging on it with a spoon, with several neighbours joining in. We then headed back inside and sang a chorus of Auld Lang Syne. It felt so good as I looked forward to the new year to come.

Our Sunday dinners, which I insisted on well after my ex left us, included my children and many of their friends. A few of them still call me Mom. Unless one was working, it was a law in our house that they all came for Sunday dinner. I am proud of each one of them, blood-related or not.

I feel so blessed to be the Nana of my three incredible grandchildren. They have always received my love to the moon and back. I was outside the delivery room when my first grandchild, my grandson, was born. My oldest daughter and son-in-law were, of course, inside the delivery room when I heard my daughter say, *I want my mom*. Well, unbeknownst to her, I was right outside the door. The doctor came out and told me that she wanted me, so I went in to meet this wonderful bundle of love lying on her chest. I never felt so blessed in my entire life! My grandson, who is now 20 years old, won my heart right then and there; I often wonder where the years went. Having a dad from India, he taught me a traditional dance, and we perform it every time we get together. Bollywood move over! We also used to yodel together just to bug his mom.

My granddaughter was the next to be born. I was living on Vancouver Island when she graced the world with her presence.

Even though I didn't meet her until she was a few months old, we have a special love connection that will never be broken. She is a beautiful girl inside and out. She calls me *Nana Cra Cra* for a good reason; we share a lot of laughter together. I remember she and her Grandpa Drew playing a game they made up when she was just a little girl. It consisted of throwing a wet washcloth at a table while sitting on lawn chairs that sat a piece away from each other. The goal was to see who could throw the washcloth the furthest. They did this for hours and then came in to watch *My Little Ponies*.

Next in line was another granddaughter. My daughter wanted me with her this time when she delivered. We tried hard but didn't make it. We were moving from the Island to Osoyoos and planned to drop our furniture off in a storage unit and proceed to our daughter in Trail the next day. We were on route and got to Manning Park when she called, saying, *Mommy, it hurts so much*. I told her that I was coming and to cross her legs. Well, we did not make it that day, so my daughter went ahead and delivered her. Typical of her - she never listens!! Besides her parents, Drew and I were the first ones to cuddle her. Although she lives four hours away, her spirit always knew us. Her Grandpop and I are always in awe of how she seems to remember us even if we do not get to see her very often. Her second name is Nicola, after my son Nicholas. He would be so proud.

My oldest daughter wrote a public tribute to me last Mother's Day:

> ***She made broken look beautiful and strong, invincible.***
> ***She walked with the Universe on her shoulders and made it look like a pair of wings.***
> ***My mom kicked so hard at the darkness it bled daylight.***

***Many times, she could have thrown in the towel and left us, but she didn't; she fought like a trooper through all life's insanities to stay with her family.
I love you Mama.***

I am forever grateful for having had the opportunity to parent such unique human beings. I did the best I could and am proud to say they forgave their father years later. My children reclaimed a relationship with him, even if it feels complicated sometimes. I was somehow able to reach deep within and become a warrior who picked up her marbles after twisting and turning around and around. I can look in the mirror and say the Universe must know what it is doing. I am more than okay now, balanced and at ease.

Holidays in our household were important occasions. I look back at happy memories of when the children were young. One Mother's Day, my two middle ones made me stay in my room until they called me to come out. When I came down the stairs from my room, they took me out to the garden where I had grown wildflowers from seed. To my astonishment, when I looked up, all that remained was a garden rake and shovel. My girl wondered why I did not initially look happy, telling me that they had cleared all the weeds out of my garden for me. I simply smiled and said, *Thank you.*

***After all, their only intention was to show me love;
new flowers could be planted,
but their precious love could never be replaced.***

I often think of Nicholas and his sister on the first Easter Sunday I spent on my own with this crew. I awoke early and helped the bunny hide the chocolates. I turned on the oven to warm, starting to get ready to cook the pies. Then, I went to wake the children for their Easter egg hunt. Suddenly, I smelled something like rubber burning. Nicholas ran into the kitchen and said, *Mommy, your Easter basket is in the oven.* Sure enough. There it was; a burned basket, dripping chocolate along with something else unidentifiable. They had both saved their allowances to buy me an Easter basket being aware that I would not get one this year. Memories like these still melt my heart.

Fast forward to Christmas; our family loved choosing our tree together. I would load the children into my car, and off we went to the tree farm. The trees were admittedly costly. I justified it because they gave free apple cider and hotdogs to eat around a campfire. Where else could I feed all eight of my children for free? This became our tradition every year.

It was insane how many presents always found their way under our tree. One year I was approached by one of my neighbours, Jill, who asked if I would be offended if the golf club her husband managed adopted our family for Christmas. I told her how nice that would be and that I was very grateful. I wasn't sure if I could do it on my own that year as I just graduated from Life Skills Coaches training and was not working yet. The golf club gave us presents from Santa and gave some for each child signed from Mom and included me on their list. As if this wasn't enough, their generosity extended to a grocery gift card for a turkey dinner.

My mother was always the original Santa, and she also went overboard that year. So, one evening, I sat having a glass of wine in front of our fireplace and thought about thinking how thankful I was. Suddenly, I was interrupted by the sound of the doorbell. Opening the door, I was greeted by the minister of the church we attended with a truck full of gifts.

He reminded me of the tree in the church that members of our congregation had filled with presents along with age and gender cards. He told me that the church chose my family to give the presents to. I was overwhelmed and surprised, and I told him how embarrassed I was as he placed the gifts under the tree. He asked me why, and I said, *Look at the number of gifts under the tree!* Looking me straight in the eye, he said, *That is how much you and your children are loved.* He put his hand on my shoulder, and I was overcome with gratitude. His words took me from a place of embarrassment to feeling totally respected – I will never forget that. It was a magical Christmas that year with over 200 gifts under the tree. It wasn't the number of presents that made our holiday so memorable, but instead, the love, respect, and kindness extended to our family. Every Christmas celebration in our home is special and never more so than that year. It was also the time of year when my wonderful son-in-law learned early in his life that if he was polite and waited until the whole gang went to the food table first, there were slim pickings left over. Of course, he was only polite and waited that first year.

So many things changed over the years, yet a lot remained the same. I continued to be the Team Mother for my oldest son's soccer team, bringing oranges and water for the boys. I cheered with all my heart at every game. Two of my sons played high school football, and I attended every game, encouraging them both with the same degree of enthusiasm.

Sports played an integral part in my children's lives, from figure skating to soccer, baseball, football, snowboarding, and basketball. My two youngest golfed as well. I believe that sports were instrumental in developing life skills and physical and mental wellness in each of them. Being on teams provided them with the opportunity to develop teamwork, leadership, critical thinking, and problem-solving skills.

I found a way to keep my children involved in activities that held their interest and gave them an outlet from some of the stress at home. When money was an issue, the schools or my parents stepped up to provide funding. We were fortunate to have many supportive people in our lives who provided these opportunities. I had to learn to ask for help, and that was a big step for me, constantly internalizing that I was worthy. Every time I reached out for help, I was amazed that someone was there to give me a hand up and more than willing to be the support I needed. Discovering resources allowed me to keep my children safe and active; they were a godsend. For example, when the high school that my son attended found out I couldn't afford the football fees, the coach called and offered to waive them. The same gesture was given when I was short for the basketball and soccer fees.

The support I thought I would receive was from those connected to my ex-husband, but many couples simply dropped me from their social circles after we divorced. His family also suddenly stepped away. I was sad because I not only lost my husband but all my nieces and nephews. However, I discovered a new support system during a time when I needed it the most, and that was all mine.

The Universe works in synchronistic ways, shown at the right moment in time.

Things have certainly changed from 20 years ago. There are now excellent support systems such as food banks, support groups like Mamas for Mamas,[1] and one-on-one counselling, as well as online support. The stigma for using these resources

---

[1] www.mamasformamas.org/

has decreased by way of the dinosaur, which is where it belongs. Over time, I learned to reach out for support when I was vulnerable; it was difficult, but I found the strength that came from deep within me. My courage came from my family income being cut off in its entirety with eight children to feed. I needed assistance and had to access different types of support, which was tough on my pride, quite honestly.

For the quickest income loss relief, I looked to the Guaranteed Income Supplement Program.[2] To my amazement, I found that there is absolutely no shame in receiving temporary help from the government. This program gave me a hand up, and I learned that it is illegal to allow your children to go hungry or become homeless, so it was not only my right but my duty as a parent to provide them with the necessities of life. I needed to show proof of income, bank account information, and a list of any other assets I owned. I was also required to provide proof of rent or mortgage and the number of children I had in addition to my identification, such as a driver's license or social insurance number. They also asked me what steps I had taken to obtain an order for support. This felt somewhat invasive. However, it was necessary to ensure I had done all I could to be granted the right to collect what my children and I needed to move forward with the application. Upon entering that office, all I felt was shame and fear, but I was determined to do everything I needed to protect my precious family. This decision saved both my life and the lives of my children. It was humbling, but this initial step changed my world for the better.

Because the Guaranteed Income Supplement Program[3] was temporary, there I was, 40 years old with no husband and

---

[2] www.canada.ca/en/services/benefits/publicpensions/cpp/old-age-security/guaranteed-income-supplement.html
[3] Ibid

my children with nowhere to turn. I hit rock bottom financially, and it took all my pride to walk through the doors of that office, which was then commonly known as welfare. I was determined to get the finances I needed so my children and I could survive. Initially, I held the misconception that only losers went on government assistance, so I berated myself and took baseball bats to my ego. My oldest daughter drove me down to the welfare office because I was shaking so badly and could not drive. When I went into the building to wait my turn to see a counsellor, I noticed quite a few young mothers with babies and older women who were seemingly as embarrassed to be there as I was. Right then and there, I changed my perception of those who had a variety of different but equally valid reasons to seek assistance. Admittedly, I did go to my parents many times in the future, and they were financially supportive. Yet, any time I went to them for money, there was an uncomfortable feeling I was begging when I asked.

The first thing my mother said when I told her that my ex had left us was, *What did you do?* This was such a slap in the face that I did not see coming. It really hurt to think that my mother assumed I was to blame. However, this should not have been a surprise to me - they were not aware of the affairs he had because I previously painted our marriage as a rosy picture. I was traumatized and took on guilt when asking for their help. Fear, desperation, and loneliness took over as I cried an ocean full of tears.

When I sat down with the woman assigned to my case, I told her the number of children I was supporting on my own with only 17 dollars in the bank. As a single mother of these many children, I knew I was doing my best, but I often felt overwhelmed, not knowing where to turn. As Charles Dickens said, *It was the best of times, it was the worst of times…*

This counsellor asked why I needed the support, so I shared that my husband left our children and me, and I had no income or recent job experience, having been a stay-at-home mom through all of my married life. I told her I had previous social work education and experience and wanted to refresh some of my courses and get back to work; I made it clear that I wanted to go back to work as soon as possible. She asked me why I wanted to do that. Thinking this was quite obvious, I replied, *To support my family.* Her response was, to say the least, non-supportive, having the audacity to state that I could stay on welfare long-term due to the age of my youngest child. Puzzled, I looked at her and reiterated that I wanted to reconnect with my career in counselling. She continued, telling me that people who say they want to be a counsellor are the ones most likely to need a counsellor. I flipped!!!

This was yet another one of those *You have got to be kidding me moments.* I had come into the welfare office with my head hung low only to be humiliated by the person in charge of supporting me. She also stated that I needed to register with the Family Maintenance Enforcement Program[4] in order to force my ex to pay child support. I already had a court order in place for this program, but foolishly, I felt bad about it as I still hoped my ex would come home as he had so many times before. Her response was, *Why would taxpayers pay what he is responsible for?* It was a good question, but I was fragile, and I hesitated to rock the boat. What I was unwilling to recognize was that the boat had already sailed.

Given how this counsellor was speaking to me, I somehow found my voice and asked to speak with her supervisor. In a private room, I told her what I had just experienced. The

---

[4] www.fmep.gov.bc.ca/

supervisor apologized profusely and said she would speak with the staff member dealing with my case. I learned two lessons that day. One is that the welfare system was flawed, and if she could call herself a counsellor and be a case manager, I could do better in my sleep. The second is that every parent has the legal obligation to attempt to have the other parent accountable financially. I also realized, without knowing it, that my recognition of her lack of skills formed the basis for my self-confidence moving forward. As a side note, this supervisor ended up working for HRDC, Human Resource Development Canada,[5] as one of my funding officers for the Project-Based Training Program, which I eventually created. After that first meeting, I knew welfare was not enough to feed, clothe, and provide daycare for my children. It was also not the legacy I wanted to leave for them.

The Family Maintenance Enforcement Program[6] provided legal aid, supporting me in my attempt to enforce my order for child support. Again, there was a legal obligation for me to pursue financial support from my ex-husband. In most cases, both parents want to provide for their children and share custody. But I found out from my lawyer that if one parent chooses to avoid their legal obligation, this program has more clout than hiring a private lawyer. The FMEP, as it is called, has the power to freeze bank accounts, garnish wages, or penalize the debtor with jail time if they refuse to pay. In some cases, a parent may hide income or use a joint bank account with someone else to avoid payment. When parents are faced with their post-separation responsibilities, the reality is that some step up and pay. However, some need to be reminded of their obligations by the court system. In my case, my ex simply did not pay or contest the order. This left my children and me

---

[5] en.wikipedia.org/wiki/Human_Resources_Development_Canada
[6] Ibid

entrenched in unworthiness, and the repercussions from this were lengthy. It was not until after he split up with his girlfriend that he opened his own account, and I was able to receive a portion of the payments owing to his children.

I was able to access a retraining program by participating in a government-funded career planning program that led me to successfully obtain the financial ability to independently provide for my family. This was an opportunity to upgrade my education and access assistance to learn new job skills. I was able to find my career using this route.

I needed to put daycare in place for when I went back to school and started working, and I found what I needed through the Guaranteed Income Supplement Program. I am grateful for the generous support I received from them for my younger children, attending the YMCA programs over the summer, as well as, before and after school programs. This program charged on a sliding scale, and I was fortunate to have this support when I needed it most, paying more when I made more. They allowed me the freedom to move forward with my education and career.

Family counselling was an excellent choice for my younger children and me. Although my family doctor could have referred me, I made my own appointment, and my counsellor charged me on a sliding scale. My ex refused to go. Making my first move toward accessing all of the support I received was a significant part of seeking personal independence and financial security. Even though it didn't feel right at the time, it was what I needed. All of these government-sponsored programs I accessed supported me financially and boosted my self-confidence. There were many times when I was totally embarrassed taking my cheque to the bank, but I kept telling myself that this was only temporary. And it was. And when that time passed, I felt strong for the first time in many months. I obtained the support I needed to move forward with my retraining and eventual employment opportunities. Someone had believed in me, and from that day on, my motto became, *Use it, do not abuse it*.

People have told me that I have two choices in life: one is to *give up*, and the other is to *step up*. I chose the latter. Ironically, this was just the first step to healing my broken spirit in a world where I longed to be worthy. I learned a big lesson here:

For me, healing did not happen through the course of time, but instead, through the intention of healing I committed to.

I had a choice to remain broken, or I could choose to heal. The universe popped up and gave me a much-needed push. Since I had the total financial and emotional responsibility for a family of nine, problem-solving became second nature. Creative budgeting also became my norm.

I had previously tried real estate, studying hard late at night after the children were asleep. I wrote the exam and got top marks, but the little girl inside me could not bear the rejection that goes hand-in-hand in that industry. Somehow, she was still there, rearing her head and invading my thoughts, and I allowed her to take over. I know that each judgment I felt was unintended to be personal, but I absorbed each one of them. I didn't sell one darn house because I did not perceive that I could be successful, and I still had hungry mouths to feed. The part of the real estate industry I enjoyed was meeting new people. However, the company I worked with believed in high-pressure sales, and I could not get on board with that. What I took away from this experience were top-notch marketing skills which I later transferred to other employment. But at this point, I was back to the drawing board.

Artwork in a park designated for ducks
to gather safely in a place of their own.
I discovered my own place after many storms
that included blood, sweat, and tears.
I feel protected by the bravery, beauty, and love
that I have come to know as my authentic self.
I am safe to be me.

VI

Finding My Wings…Ready to Fly

After leaving real estate, a friend of mine urged me to look at different options for employment. I chose to take a course at the Academy of Learning in career planning. I went into it confused, figuring that since it was a computer school, the focus would be on computers. However, that was not what I applied for. I stuck it out, finding support from one heck of a career coach. Tanis was one of the many guardian angels in my life.

    She led me through exercises that helped me identify my skill set and look at areas that were weaknesses. I did not have any computer skills, and I needed training in order to write proposals and lesson plans. I believed I was a planner because I had to make lists and time schedules managing a family of eight children. Tanis pointed out that was probably not part of my true personality. She firmly believed I was a risk-taker and a *fly by the seat of my pants* kind of girl. That didn't sink in at first. Every morning before the children woke up, I organized and planned. I was flexible to daily changes but organizing all my day's activities was a must. I came to discover she was right, and my children agree. I have learned that circumstances made me a planner, yet it is not my true soul. When my children were young and at home, I had to plan for the many different activities our family was involved in. And now, I have to plan my meals and other wellness practices for health reasons. But I have to agree with Tanis; it is a learned behaviour - I can do both, but I prefer to take risks and be more spontaneous in life.

I thought I would like to work in the legal field as a secretary. Tanis didn't say much, but we went through the testing, job market research, and transferring skills, the whole shebang. Then one day, she asked me to come into her office to sit down with me *for a chat* as she put it. This became a life-changing meeting. We discussed all my skill sets, which indicated pointing me towards me becoming a coach. I looked at her completely dumbfounded. Coaching was what I had studied but never practiced and what I expressed interest in when I met my case manager at the welfare office. The next thing I knew, I was in a mock interview provided by the owner of the Academy of Learning. It went so well that he told Tanis he wanted me to manage the life skills Project Based Training at the school. It became obvious that, while the other students engaged in a mock interview, mine was the real deal.

Tanis suggested I take a 3-month life coaching course downtown to update my skills; once complete, I would be hired. *Hmm*, I said to myself. But I agreed, even though I did not know what on earth a life skills coach was. I decided I had nothing to lose - I would fly by the seat of my pants, thinking, *what the heck*. Years later, Tanis and I had a good chuckle over this. She told me there was no way I could have worked as a legal secretary. She said I would have tried to coach the computer and counsel the clients before seeing the lawyer. That is probably true!

In my mind, the life coaching school I attended was toxic. I thought it was poorly run and emotionally dangerous for those attending. As a life skills coach, I would never be willing to do the things they were advocating with my clients. I was relieved to hear that they closed shortly after I finished the program.

I used to hang out with a particular fellow student during

lunch. We would go to the mall and get a hotdog, and after several weeks, I gave him my phone number. Shortly after, one of the coaches called me into her office. She told me that the man I gave my phone number to was on parole and living in a group home after serving time for murdering his wife. He and I talked about a lot of things … mostly about me. I can really talk. In retrospect, I realize that he never gave me much information about himself. The teachers told him not to call me, and he did not. Maybe I should have been a little less chatty and a little more attentive. Oops. So much for my taste in men. I believe in giving people second chances, but this situation could have jeopardized my children and me; I could have lost more than my marbles! I called Tanis night after night, wanting to quit that program. Funny that I needed her permission to tell the little girl in me to keep going.

Looking back, I just wanted someone to tell me to hang in. She told me to play the game. Her advice was, *Just get your damn certificate because you'll have a job at the end of this. Learn what not to do as a life coach, and then do it your way.* So, after three long months of training that I did not believe in and where I felt disingenuous, I graduated. I was impressed that I made it through the tortures of this school's dynamics. My core values did not align with their teachings because I believe strongly in empathy and respect for others, and I saw none of that in their program. Despite the odds, and while fighting my integrity, I learned a lot and proceeded to provide tools for others with clear intentions while creating a program based on quality care, mutual trust and inclusion.

With the help of the Academy of Learning, I was able to gain some basic computer skills. I am not at all tech-savvy, and I struggle, even today. Upon hiring me for the Project-Based Training Program, I remember the owner, Don, saying that I could enroll in my choice of computer programs for free. Well, that was interesting! I didn't know which one to choose first because all I knew about computers was that they were beige. He said, *I think you should start with this*, and handed me a floppy disc. I sat at the computer station feeling stupid; I didn't even know where the disc went! After what seemed like an hour, he came back and asked what was wrong. I handed him the disc and told him I didn't know where to put it. He laughed so hard and showed me where to insert the disc saying, *This will be much more difficult than I thought*. Eventually, I learned how to use the Microsoft Word program, and off I went.

I was a total wreck the day I met my first students. It started as a half-day group session until the existing coach finished his contract. This was a practicum placement as I had not officially graduated yet. Tanis and I spoke before I went into the classroom. I will never forget what she said to me that day, looking me straight in the eyes as I shook with nerves before her…

> ***Don't be selfish; you have so much to give.***
> ***If you make a difference in one person's life in there,***
> ***you will have made a world of a difference.***

With her words ringing in my ears, I carried on without a clue what I was doing. I saw the outline of the current program, and it made me shutter. Here was a man leading a group of women who were self-identified victims of domestic violence. Although he was qualified, could that be any more insane? Strangely enough, it gave me the courage to put myself out there. Instinctively, I knew I could do better. I became very connected to these women, and in a few weeks, I took over the group. I graduated knowing that if I was going to be a motivational and supportive coach, I had to learn my own way within it. I turned my program into one that assisted students in the development of personal management skills, rewriting the script and designing the program. I did the intake, and I personally created every lesson plan. For many hours at home on my computer, I researched site after site with various types of personal management skills. I designed my versions of mind-mapping, setting goals, and recognizing how to access effective areas of support for my students. I practised by talking to the fireplace, and I am confident anyone looking in would defiantly say I had completely lost it. However, this was where my passion lay, and I enjoyed every minute of it. Creating the *New Beginnings* program fed into my leadership skills and love of facing challenges head-on.

My students were immigrants who had worked in Canada for a short period of time but were unsuccessful in maintaining employment due to a language barrier and were receiving employment insurance. My students worked in various professions in their home country but could not work in their field without costly retraining here in Canada. Most had young families, so the length of time needed to get licenses or degrees was daunting and financially unrealistic. Their level of speaking English varied, but all were able to understand the written word at a high level of competency. Case managers in HRDC referred clients they thought would benefit from the program, and then I hand-picked the participants. I based my groups on two criteria. First and foremost, I obtained a sense of what level of English they possessed and chose each student dependent on the likelihood of their ability to communicate within a specific group. I did this piece in conjunction with the ESL - English as a Second Language – teacher I hired. The second criterion was their level of motivation. I required them to be excited about this opportunity to gain new skills to obtain and maintain careers after program completion. In addition, the ESL teacher and I provided them with an opportunity to develop English language enunciation at a higher level. I am proud to say this was very successful. One hundred percent of my groups stayed the course of the program and graduated. I had funding officers come in for surprise visits, during which I left the room. At one point, Georgio, one of the funding officers, came out and said, *Just once, Dorri, just once, I want to come out of the room with them not telling me how much they love you.* I smiled and said *I love them too.* And I meant it.

I created my lesson plans based loosely on material from Steven Covey's *7 Habits of Highly Effective People.* I took some of his ideas and developed my versions. The program had lesson plans that included identifying individual core values, managing stress, self-care, anger management, goal setting, and mind-mapping. We also taught subjects that included Canada's Human Rights, The Employment Standards Act and Work Safe BC. I also based another portion on my students acquiring skills in career planning and job searching. Tanis was such a role model and mentor that I became fully prepared in both of these areas. It was a unique program because I did not copy anyone else's agendas or materials; my lesson plans were my own, and they were often were student-led. Sometimes they suggested what they wanted to see in the next lesson plan, and there were times when I went with it, adapting to group interest and perceived need. I believed if I chose a group of like-minded individuals, lesson plans would flow and conversations would be natural. I did not lecture but instead led. We all participated as the goal was to combine subject discussion with practical speaking opportunities. We had our fun as well. I remember asking my students to write a three-minute speech on any topic they chose. Many chose life from their home countries, and I felt so connected with them and their stories.

My students spent the afternoon with the ESL teacher while I conducted one-on-one counselling sessions that were client-led. We spoke of a variety of issues depending on individual client needs. Many spoke of their homelands and what they had left behind. Some were grieving lost relatives and careers given up, and I was the ear they needed. Others had relationship challenges, and some suffered from a form of PTSD from what they had witnessed back home. One of my students often almost jumped out of her seat if she heard a car backfire. With terror in her eyes, she described her memories from a war-torn country. I cannot imagine how much she had survived.

Another beautiful soul came to Canada as a mail-order bride. At first, her husband was very attentive, showering her with gifts and outings to high-end restaurants. Things suddenly changed for her when she found out he had a drug addiction and forced her to prostitute herself to provide money for his drugs. If she complained, he beat her. I spoke with her case manager, and together, we devised a plan to get her to a safe house. I actually bumped into her years later, and she was pushing a baby stroller with a newborn baby inside. Smiling broadly, she told me that she had met and married a great man and her life was good.

I love happy endings.
I learned so much from my students.
They confided their hopes and dreams
for the future with me;
I felt very blessed that I held their trust and respect.

Computer classes were given over the next three months by the facilitators at the Academy of Learning with whom I partnered. I continued my one-on-one sessions and obtained practicum placements for the end of the program. At the completion of each group, we held a buffet luncheon where the students brought a plate from their homeland that we all shared. They each had a chance to say a few words about what they were taking away from the course, New Beginnings, and share their hopes going forward. It always touched my soul that they showed such gratitude and excitement for the new prospects that lay ahead.

Several of my students were hired by the companies with which I had placed them for practicums. I was so happy that 85 percent of my students found permanent jobs and maintained employment three years after the program ended. I followed up with group participants, and their thankfulness for the opportunities this program provided them was overwhelming at times, but in a great way. I felt I had accomplished what I set out to do and more.

An interesting fact is how, even with the diversity of the group - age, gender, and culture - I always sensed they were an inclusive group. Perhaps the commonality of being new immigrants, what they had gone through, and what they had left behind bonded them in such a way that discouraged any division. I believe they all held similar goals and had each other's backs. Being such a support to one another was a testament to their deep understanding of overcoming adversity. It was fulfilling to motivate such fine people who could withstand so much and come out on the other side in their new country with exciting goals and dreams yet to be fulfilled.

Somewhere along the road, the little girl in me found a place where she belonged. She was no longer a negative presence in my life. Although she still visits my thoughts from time to time, I have learned to respect her for the most part with self-confidence taking a front seat. I believed in myself for once in my life… and I got paid for it. Remembering when I received my first paycheque, I could not believe I had so much fun working at a job where I combined my creative skills with my counselling abilities. This new me exceeded my expectations. I felt deeply alive, believing that the universe put opportunities in front of me. I remained open and did not put up barriers that could have prevented me from moving forward. I believed I could succeed, and I did.

I believe that the great moments of my life are not usually found within big events. They happened for me when I was able to see myself take risks that paid off. I listened when someone told me they believed in me, and I embraced a simple hug when I didn't even know I needed one. When a student in my program thanked me for making a difference in their life, I was honoured for having had the opportunity. I am humbled to this day by the trust and faith these amazing humans gave me. I suppose at the end of the day, we all grew together. This taught me that, to begin healing to become the best I could be, it was essential that I remain true to my values and moral authenticity. I gave what was genuine, and I received 110 percent back.

I was nominated and received the Self-Sufficiency Award in 1996 awarded by the government, an honour which I will never forget. There was part of me that still thinks back and says, *Wow girl, you did it!* And another part makes me step back with humility. This award provided a top-up to my salary, which meant I could stop relying on anyone but myself to provide for my children and me. I do not know who nominated me, but whoever it was, is my unsung hero.

The people and places who were there to offer an opportunity while believing in me empowered me to enrich the lives of those I love the most - my family, my students, and eventually, myself. To get to a place of loving myself took a lot of courage and internal work. I realized I couldn't give what I did not have, and I finally became healthy. I learned to love myself more deeply, and as a result, I could openly connect with others. That placed me in the best spot to give.

After the government funding ended, the Project-Based Training Program did as well, and I found myself unemployed and needing to look at future employment options. I had created and delivered the program, New Beginnings, for over seven years; it was my baby, but I had to let it go. This time, I knew what I had to offer and began my job search. This wasn't as easy as I thought. The coach in me had to look back and put into practice what she taught. It was not an easy month. I still had a family to support and mouths to feed, so I had to find a job as soon as possible. I did not have the luxury of not working, and my insecurities crept back in. So, I sent out my resumes, and one job offer came up. It was a position that paid less money, but it looked like something I could do for the time being. The hiring committee told me that the program was being developed to assess and help qualify immigrants for training opportunities funded by the federal government. They were bringing in a woman who had assisted in the set-up of the same program in Victoria. Once the program was set up, she would leave, and I would carry on in that position. When Lorraine was set to leave, the position was posted, even though I was told I was the one to take over. I requested a meeting with the department head and asked her what happened and why she changed her mind. Her answer was simple, *You aren't suitable. You wear your heart on your sleeve.* That was enough for me to recognize that this work environment was not for me. She clearly did not recognize what I had to offer.

The person who did get the position soon became one of my best friends. Catherine Ewing inspired me to become more than I thought I could be. She still touches my soul. This wonderful human being is one of the most caring, authentic, giving people I have ever had the pleasure of meeting. She is definitely a hero to me. Her professionalism under pressure inspired me. Catherine taught me to honour my unique gifts and never allow anyone to take away my positive fighting spirit. She introduced me to a bunch of like-minded friends on Hay House, a chat room where we gathered most evenings. I was addicted.

I went by the name Angel because that was the name my mother called me, and Catherine called me *Angelsnot*, which was much more in line with my true personality. These online chats provided me with a much-needed place to go to feel connected to the outside world. To this day, I have the privilege of remaining friends with many of the wonderful people I met there, including Cath. This is a group of fantastic women and men from all over the world who make me laugh, inspire me, and when I have my back to the wall, they are there with their hearts open and words of encouragement.

Catherine and I held *Heart Attack Wednesdays*, where the two of us ordered hamburgers from Wendy's dripping with fried onions, mushrooms, bacon, and cheese. Just thinking about these gives me the warm fuzzies. I also had the absolute honour and privilege to work with John De Freitas, the driving force behind convincing me to write this book. These two wonderful people have supported me through life's battles and shown me that friendships can lie dormant for years and then spring back when you least expect them to. So even in an office run by politics and favouritism, a bright light managed to shine through every experience. This proved to me that, even though I went through dark times and periods of perceived loss, I could always calm the storm by recognizing a lesson awaited; there was always an opportunity to get what I needed with a change in perception.

As this proved to be a very political workplace where I was not valued, I saw an ad for an employment coordinator on a First Nations reservation and applied. The department head who rejected me for having too big a heart applied for the same position. She was now rejected, and I got the job. Karma can be a bitch.

Enter my employment with an Indigenous reserve on the lower mainland. I applied for the position of Employment Development Counselor and, *surprisingly*, got the job. I say surprisingly because I went into the interview not having a clue about Indigenous life on a reserve or the ARDA - Aboriginal Regional Development Agreement - that I was to run for the band. I admitted this at the interview and never expected a callback. I received a call two weeks later, being appointed by Chief and Council for the position if I agreed. This was another one of many *you have got to be kidding moments*. But hey, here I went again.

This was another position I went into, flying by the seat of my pants. I virtually knew nothing about the cultural practices and challenges of the band, but I was soon to gain a tremendous amount of knowledge. It wasn't easy not being Indigenous and working on a reservation - I was resented by many. The Chief and I got along exceptionally well, and most of the council members were very supportive. Although hired as the Employment Development Coordinator, I transitioned into being the Director of Recreation and Youth. I was also assigned to work with the Economic Development Department because I signed a contract that stated *other duties as assigned*. I found out very quickly what that meant. On an Indigenous reservation, one wears many hats.

I helped design and put a breakfast club into place for school-aged children. Some children went to school hungry, while others had parents who made them a nutritious breakfast every day. I worked with the Social Development Department to ensure that all children received a healthy daily breakfast. We opened it up to all the kids on the reserve to not embarrass the child who needed the meal support the most. I also personally put together lunches and delivered them twice a week to the school off the reserve. There was no funding for this, so I needed to be creative and hired staff to cook, clean up, and purchase the food from the Employment Development Department funds. I had to think outside the box while simultaneously passing every government audit with flying colours. I was motivated by my creativity when faced with a challenge, so it was a win-win for everyone.

I put several Targeted Wage Subsidy Agreements in place both on and off the reserve. These were designed to attract businesses like the art gallery, carving artists, jewellery-makers, and the gift shop to hire clients with limited or no work experience.

My first assistant helped me gain the Elders' trust by driving me around to their homes to introduce me. She was from a prominent band family, and her seal of approval meant I had an ally. The acceptance of the Elders was vital in my ability to run my departments; they welcomed me, and I appreciated their support. Initially, my office was in a portable outside of the main office, and I loved the fact that I could run my program my way. Most of my clients were between the ages of 19 and

29, so I made the portable user-friendly. I put on current music and turned up the tunes just the way they liked it. I also went outside for a smoke with them, which put them at ease. This allowed me to talk freely about any number of their concerns and further determine their job readiness. When I eventually moved into the main office, many felt intimidated, so they stopped dropping in. I convinced the Chief that I needed to go back to the portable, and she agreed.

I cannot say everyone favoured a non-indigenous person making decisions on behalf of the band members. I faced discrimination from many of them. I was called *too white* and *too HRDC*, meaning I represented the government. But I kept my composure, knowing my intent was genuine, wanting the best for everyone involved. However, there were times when these remarks hurt me deeply through the disconnection created as a result. There were judgments made responding to a difference of opinion about how I allotted funds within the budget and funding decisions. Being a small reservation of 350 residents, everyone was aware of decisions made, and many voiced their opinions. But I was in charge of the departments and needed to make those decisions based on what I thought was right for the band as a whole. I became very wise about de-escalating situations and putting out fires, standing firm without letting opinions sway me. Being fully transparent, I joined in laughing at a few jokes told by Indigenous people about Indigenous people and was told I was prejudice - I learned a lot about myself and others working there.

I remember one angry young man I accompanied into Richmond so he could write his driver's license test. Every time his name came up, he slipped outside for a smoke, putting him to the back of the line. I was livid, spending my time there with him for nothing. So, I pulled him outside and said, *Okay, let's go, Kevin; I've had enough.* He became even angrier, but I told him he needed to get in my car immediately if he wanted a drive back to the reserve, . He begrudgingly obliged, swearing at me the whole way back. When we arrived on the reserve, I went into my office, picked up some of my things and went home for the night. The next morning when I got to my office portable, Kevin came in and asked if we could talk. I said, *Sure, have a seat.* He told me that he wanted to apologize to me about the day before. My response was a bit guarded, *Okay?* He put his head in his hands and then looked me straight in the eye. He explained that what he did wasn't personal. He told me that he was acting out of built-up frustration and continued to share that he had recently returned from living on the streets of Vancouver. He was back to help his mother and father raise his two youngest siblings. There was a history of drugs and abuse in the family. He continued to tell me that he had a tough 24 hours the day before his driver's test, and he took it out on me. My words in response to him were, *If you are up to it, why don't we try again*, and we did. He went on to get his license and then worked on the reserve as the maintenance worker. This gave him money to help at home and a sense of pride contributing to the community.

> **When I left my employment there,**
> **he came up to me with tears in his eyes**
> **and thanked me, telling me that I changed his life.**
> **We shared a big hug,**
> **and I had tears in my eyes as I left the reserve.**

My second assistant was a young girl and mother who won my heart. She worked hard both at home and in the office. She knew many of the reserve's young people and was my constant ally. She and I collaborated on most of the decisions I made because I valued her opinion from a band member's perspective. She laughed at my filing abilities, which was, admittedly, not one of my greatest assets. I was lost using Excel, and she set me up with the formulas to create the budgets. I was adamant that when I left, she would be considered as the one to succeed me. My biggest hope was to pass my knowledge on running these departments to a band member. This would provide the band with the knowledge I shared about government funding protocols and create more diversity inclusive of cultural practices and norms. I had mentioned this to the Chief when we went to a retreat in Banff, telling her my intentions. She was surprised and asked me why I would talk myself out of a job. I think she was equally surprised when I told her I would give myself three years to find and train someone from the band to take over. As it turned out, it was just a few months shy of three years when I left to move to Vancouver Island, paving the way for my assistant to take my place. This young woman enrolled in job search coaching at night without my knowledge until she came in one day with her certificate. I was very impressed. I had the funding in our budget to repay her for the course, with which I surprised her. It was right then and there I knew I was right; she was the one to take over when I left, and she did.

I had a lot of fun working on this job. I also learned many parts of the Indigenous culture and the people of this band. I recall the time some of the members of the band tried to teach me the rain dance. We had a great time, and I made the moves the best I could. The very next morning, we woke up to a blizzard, a snowstorm that blanketed the reserve. You can well imagine the teasing I got when I went back to work with the Chief saying, *That is what we get for teaching a white girl to dance!!*

A totem pole project I funded through my department was extremely meaningful. Each piece of the totem pole held significance and shared a story. The master carver was respected, and his students studied the woodwork and the discipline to follow his lead. They learned the meaning of each piece - this was their history, and they owned it through their carving. Following up on my funding programs, I gained the knowledge that the creation of a totem pole was priceless.

I was taught cultural etiquette while interacting with one particular Elder on the reserve. Even though everyone had a landline telephone, if I wanted to reach them for any reason, I was to go directly to their home as a sign of respect. I made the mistake once of calling one of the Elders to ask him to play Santa Claus at the Christmas party and was rebuked. I needed to apologize and ask him in person.

One spring morning, with the mist of the ocean covering the fields, I arrived at work to see two wolves. This was not a common occurrence. It was mystical as I experienced the majestic energy of these animals. They came right up to my car. No one was around since I arrived early that day. I sat completely still as they looked at me and I at them. There was no way I was going to be the first to make a move. After a short time, I suppose they got bored looking at me and trotted off into the fields. When I shared this with one of the Elders, she told me I was wise because the wolves came to honour me as a teacher. To this day, when there is a full moon, I feel the urge to look to the sky and howl.

The Big House was where they gathered a long time ago in the winter to share warm fires, shelter, food, and stories. They stayed there until the spring. This has changed as they all have homes of their own and only gather there for special occasions and spiritual activities. It was an honour to be invited to a couple of gatherings in The Big House.

I discovered that women living on the reservation do not always have an easy life. They face discrimination while trying hard to get back to their roots, and many face domestic abuse. They lack the same resources that Indigenous women who live off the reserve receive. Mental health support is non-existent, and there are no food banks. My first assistant refused to go with me off the reserve because she felt people stared at and judged her for who she was. She was right. For lack of better words, the surrounding town was made up of primarily white people, many of whom showed up as entitled. When I managed to convince my assistant to go into town with me for lunch, I encouraged her to hold her head up, ignore them, and enjoy her meal. I used our outings as an opportunity to support her to be confident and proud of who she is.

Some people on the reserve teach their native language to others, and some make jewelry and paint. Some have also gone on to university. The women here were diverse as in any community with varied schooling levels, hobbies, talents, and reservation roles. I enjoyed the Elders' lunches, to which all staff and band members were invited. I was introduced to bannock, deer meat, and ooligans, the first fish of the spring. I made the mistake of calling them hooligans, and the Chief laughed and told me, *Those are your children, Dorri!* These lunches were a wonderful place to learn about their history, and they always accepted me as one of the community members.

I witnessed first-hand how residential schools had a significant impact on the way parents brought up their children. Having been deprived of family life while attending these schools, many had gaps in their parenting knowledge and skills. I listened to stories of being torn away from their families and placed in residential schools, with priests and nuns becoming their role models. Women were expected to parent the way their forefathers did, and they lacked the knowledge and skills to do so. They lost all knowledge of their culture at such a young age when forced into schools designed to do just that. Many of their children were left to be brought up on their own, and their culture suffered greatly. Some turned to drugs and alcohol to avoid the pain. They had to relearn their native tongue and Indigenous ways. All they ever wanted was respect for their practices and the culture and history of their people.

Chief and Council asked me to look into building a safehouse on or off the reserve for women who felt afraid of their partners and needed assistance with their children. So, I held community focus groups consisting of band women living on the reserve. I invited these women to voice their opinion on what type of assistance was needed, where to locate it, and if developed, what it would look like. In total, I believe there were eight weekly sessions where the women became more and more engaged in discussions, and this gave me a good picture of what they wanted to see and support. After these sessions, I reported all findings to the Chief and Council. They asked me to get in touch with possible funders, and at the request of the Chief, to partner up with another band, which I did. I hired my friend Catherine as the project funding proposal writer to help me. Unfortunately, for whatever reason, it was not implemented before l retired to Vancouver Island.

I learned so much, and I am ever so grateful for the time spent working on the reserve. When I hear about systemic racism today, I can understand more deeply than if I never had this experience. I see with empathy how injustice affects people of different cultures and can be divisive. I have a greater understanding of why this exists in the Indigenous world and how change only occurs by listening with the intention to understand instead of talking about change without discovering its purpose.

    I did a lot by flying by the seat of my pants into unknown territory with the perception that I could do it with the intent of getting it done. I believe the universe put opportunities in front of me. I was open and took advantage of them to move forward. Listening to my inner voice allowed me to experience life using my gut instinct, and in most cases, it did not fail me. With each step along the way, I recognized what I was capable of, and I changed. I held my head up high and walked with a light step and a loving heart through my personal evolution. I was brave, smart, and strong. All my experiences, good and bad, lead me to this place in my life, embracing it from a different perspective; it reiterates the worthy person I know I am.

> ***It has been said that***
> ***"Strength comes from the storms we go through***
> ***and the madness we survive."*** [8]

    In my case, that could not be truer. I stopped people-pleasing and learned to value what I had to contribute and hold fast to my truth.

---

[8] Unknown

This is a twisted angel my grandson gave to me
when he was just little.
The angel resonates with finding my strength to trust in the
universe enough to fly by the seat of my pants into a career
that supported my family financially and allowed me to
discover and honour my own inner spirit.
I could then share my gifts with others
which gave me great joy.
I took my wings and flew in the face of adversity, and I won.

VII

Island life

In 2003, I received the once-in-a-lifetime gift of someone who believes in me and loves me unconditionally. Enter my husband, Drew. Our personalities are total opposites. His mind is engineered towards logic and math, while I am the spur of the moment, let's see what happens, kind of girl. I am messy, and he is one of the most organized people I have ever met. I enjoy spending money; Drew likes saving it. This works for both of us as we keep each other in check. I am energized through social interaction, and my dear husband is happiest enjoying time with our children or just the two of us.

Like most couples, we've had our disagreements. However, both of us have learned to compromise and respect the other's point of view. I think from my heart and base my decisions on my emotions. On the other hand, Drew deals with facts – he is my Ying, and I am his Yang. We healthily balance each other, relish our friendship and trust our love for each other.

Drew works away in camps for weeks at a time, and this has been hard on me. I am used to having people and admit this is something I am still working on. I hear the little girl playing in my mind with thoughts producing fear that he will not return and I am being abandoned. My abandonment issues are rooted far deeper than I thought, so it makes sense that I would try to transfer these to someone else within another relationship. At the very least, I can now recognize where they come from and where they do and don't belong. It always amazes me that the

Universe offers opportunities to heal when the time is right. Drew would not let me stay hiding under the stone that still presents moments to crush me. He recognized early in our relationship that I still had healing to do, and he has been *my rock*. He helped me pick up the broken pieces and become who I am freely meant to be. He is my hero and my number one supporter, thankfully, no matter what I do. Oh, and he sighs a lot!

Drew and I have learned to deal with constantly living apart and then coming back together, along with issues as they arise. I am still very unhappy when he leaves. However, after a few days, I get used to being on my own and doing things my way. And then he comes home, and bam, the dynamics change.

Working in camp for weeks, sometimes a month at a time is good for him; he loves what he does. Somehow, we make it work, but I'm not always comfortable with being home alone. This has created some division in our relationship. I see his point - he is excellent at what he does, often being headhunted by companies, but that doesn't discount that I am often left at home, feeling lonely. I am not unique in this. Many wives of camp-employed men experience the same.

> ***My fears of abandonment are only in my mind,***
> ***and while Drew understands this, it is my work to do, not his.***

Years ago, Drew worked in Klemtu at a fish farm. I had the opportunity to fly there with Drew by seaplane to see the area with his boss and a gentleman from head office. The majority of workers on the farm were Indigenous from the Kitasoo band. We arrived at the airport in Coal Harbour just as it began to snow. I wore a pair of white open-back sneakers, which were stylish but sure didn't cut it from a functionality point of view.

There was some time to spare before take-off, and I chatted with the man from head office. We shared a few laughs, mainly about my choice of footwear.

Finally, Drew's boss arrived. I was a bit nervous as I had never been on a seaplane before. Drew told me his boss mentioned that the man from head office was a very important person. I took this as a challenge, not being deterred by that fact. So, just after take-off, I turned to the man I just met and said *I hear you are a very important person. We should get along just great as I'm a very important person too.* The look on Drew's boss's face was priceless, and the man from head office just howled. Once we arrived, I was escorted into the cabin where everyone slept and ate. I surmised that I was to sleep there too, and Drew and I shared a bunk bed. I took the top because, as a child, I always wanted to sleep in an upper bunk. After being introduced to the men, we went to the village of Klemtu by boat. We were invited into The Long House and welcomed by the Elders. One of the most revered Elders told us about the history of the Kitasoo band. He also pointed to me and said, *I heard you are a very important person as well.* We all got a big laugh out of that. That is what they call the moccasin telegraph - word travels fast on reservations.

I spend the rest of the week fixing supper for the men who worked in the camp. There were only about six plus me, so it wasn't that hard. In the evenings, we sat around the cabin, and they told me tales about the history of their native culture, including the Kermode bear - the Sasquatch, or Big Foot as they called this spirit bear. I cooked all the suppers, and as a reward, they spent time with me explaining Klemtu and the Kitasoo band. It was a fascinating week filled with sharing and trust. It was an honour to be in their presence.

When we first met, Drew was an avid boater. I, on the other

hand, got seasick on the ferry. Back then, he told me, *Well, if we do get serious, you will spend a lot of time at home alone as I am out every weekend on the boat.* At the time, he owned a 26-foot boat that slept four. He lived on Vancouver Island, and I lived on the Lower Mainland. Here I go again, I thought. But I kind of like him, so I thought I would give it a try. I didn't think it would be a big stretch because I am a strong swimmer who always loved being at the lake and believed this could not be much different. Boy, this was an eye-opener.

I remember stepping onto the dock where the boat was moored and thinking, *This doesn't look too hard.* Two of Drew's friends joined us, and we were thrilled that it turned out to be a sunny day with calm ocean waters. Off we went and, incredibly, I did not feel nauseous at all and thoroughly enjoyed the company. That was until the weather changed and the ocean showed who the master was. The swells were enormous; I had never seen waves so dangerous, and all my happy-go-lucky feelings went overboard. I sat on the back deck, clinging to my chair as the boat rocked from side to side, alternating rolling over some waves and propelling air born over others. I simply screamed until I had no breath left. I honestly thought I was going to die. One of Drew's friends came to my rescue and calmly shared his trust in Drew and his boating experience. His wife was up on the bridge with Drew yelling *Whee* with every wave! *Oh my goodness,* I thought, *We have all gone mad.* In the words of Meatloaf *There's always something magic, there's always something new.*

But this wasn't rock and roll,
and I wasn't sure I liked this kind of magic
or if I would live to see any of my dreams come true.

Finally, after what seemed an eternity, Drew docked the boat, and we got off for a reprieve from the storm. Amazingly, I was not sick but still suffered from extreme fear. The rocking continued for over a day, yet Drew managed to conquer the waves and hold the boat steady through it all. I decided to try again and put my faith in him, even though I believed I had simply lost my marbles. Looking back, I owe him and his friends a debt of gratitude; it was a huge learning curve for me and an important one moving forward in my relationship with my husband.

A couple of weeks later, we looked at buying a house on the island where he lived. He worked for the Government at the time, and I still worked on the reservation on the mainland. This move would mean a big change for me and my children. I would be leaving my job and packing up with two teenagers in tow. Needless to say, my son and daughter were not happy campers, and my daughter resisted the move as much as she could.

Nevertheless, we found a wonderful house in Campbell River overlooking the ocean, and we moved in a month later. Drew was so excited. For one thing, the house had an ice-making fridge… there were other attractive features, but that is what he was the most excited about!

It was not an easy move, having to persuade the children I still had at home in Richmond, and I needed to give up my career. I was determined to make this new lifestyle work with many tears and angry words spoken between my children and me. If I hadn't lost my marbles on that boat, they thought I had now!! I believed in my heart that my two teenagers would come to embrace island life as much as I had. The changes were significant for all of us. Incredibly we all got through it together.

My daughter joined the basketball team, and, just as in Richmond, she excelled. Finding her best friend helped my daughter through the transition while my son turned to basketball and football. Like his brother, Nicholas, he was a very skilled football player, winning MVP in his senior year. He has many friends from the island who he still keeps in contact with. It was a successful move for everyone, but as in all times of change, it had its moments. My daughter currently lives in Richmond with her best friend from the island; she often returns for a visit to connect with other friends she made. I know she would love it if we returned to live on the island again, but that isn't in the cards for us.

So many nights were spent with Drew lighting up the BBQ on our back deck, slinging hamburgers and hot dogs for the football team. The guys played pool and cards downstairs in our games room. They also liked to soak in the hot tub. Some of them, especially those who played defence, were not small, so to be safe, Drew reinforced our hot tub. He asked the boys if they could bring something when they gathered at our home as we supplied everything else. Once, one of them brought bacon. I still laugh at the look on Drew's face when he handed it to him. Those were good times and good memories. I felt my world was finally and completely at peace.

Eventually, our children moved back to Richmond after completing their high school diplomas. It was then that Drew said, *Let's look at living on a boat.* But by this time, I had my sea legs, so I figured why not.

We were married in July, 2005 on the beach at Rebecca Spit on Quadra Island in an intimate ceremony with only ten guests. The officiant was from the Cree Nation and incorporated the Feather Ceremony into our wedding. Despite the fact that Drew doesn't like to be the center of attention, we both had fun. We played croquette, ate a catered picnic lunch, and left on our boat - probably not a typical wedding, but neither are we. This officiant went on to perform the marriage of one of my daughters at Heriot Bay on Quadra Island several years later.

Our home sat on the market for quite a while. However, we were not in a hurry, so we didn't worry. Our realtor suggested painting our great room a taupe colour. We discovered that taupe comes in many different colour variations. Drew chose the colour, and off he went, painting his heart out. I was kind. I didn't say anything, but to me it was purple instead of the brownish colour I had envisioned. It was bad. He actually woke up in the middle of the night telling me that he dreamt he was trapped in a grape and needed to escape. We also changed some carpeting to hardwood and laid it ourselves; the place sold for a good profit. At one of our open houses, a woman asked why we were selling, and I told her that my husband wanted to live on a boat. She jokingly told me that I should sell my husband and keep the house. I thought she might have a point because *You have got to be flipping kidding me* once again through my mind when he first proposed his idea. But this was Drew's lifelong dream, and after thinking about it, I agreed; why not!! I had wanted an adventure, and here it was. I was excited to start something new and challenging - life was never boring.

In 2006, after selling our house, Drew went down to Florida to look at boats while I attended a business planning course put on by HRDC. He brought our mid-sized yacht christened Mirage back to Victoria. I asked if we could change the name, but I found out it is considered bad luck to do this, so it remained the same. I must say I came a long way from the girl who got seasick on the ferries to living aboard a boat. Mirage was almost 50 feet from bow to stern and had all the amenities of a floating condominium. She had satellite TV and internet, as well as a built-in stereo system. There were two staterooms, in-suite bathrooms with showers, and a built-in ice cube maker, which, of course, Drew loved. He put in an apartment-sized refrigerator and bought a convection oven. I found out that everything on the boat had to be built in. Our washer and dryer, as well as our vacuuming system, was incorporated into the boat. I felt comfortable almost immediately, which was good because our house was sold, and this was now my home.

I lived with Drew in many places around the West Coast on board our yacht. Our first home base was the dock in Victoria, BC. Drew brought the boat up from Florida to Victoria, where we secured moorage in front of the Empress Hotel. The city of Victoria is beautiful, and we were right in the heart of downtown. Drew spent many days getting the boat back in shape after being trucked up from the States. They were to have winterized it, but when it came up, the agents in Florida did not have a clue how to do that. So, the first thing on Drew's list was to get a new hot water tank as the old one had frozen.

We spent several months moored across from the Empress. It was early February and looking out over the harbour with the hotel lit up at night provided a sense of calm and wonder. However, in the spring, the boats that people lived aboard had to be moved to Wharf Street to allow tourist boats to use the space. It was more eclectic at these docks at Warf Street with ships of every description; old, new, and every size, colour, and shape.

Our slip was situated right up against the parking lot of a local bar - that proved interesting, to say the least. During the day, a homeless community gathered to spend time in the parking lot. We had our pug on board, and Charlie and I often walked by that area. Many became somewhat attached to Charlie, and it was nice to see their faces light up when I took him over to them to be pet. I always felt happy, bringing a little sunshine into their lives.

When we went to bed at night, the music from the bar played off in the distance, so no worries. However, one hour before closing time every night, the music ramped up, fights began outside, and then, we heard police sirens. It wasn't called the *Boom Boom Room* for nothing. It occurred every night, and we asked the harbour master to move us. I never really felt afraid, but it sure didn't help me get a good sleep.

Our third slip was at Fisherman's Warf. This was a very tourist-friendly spot in Victoria. We were supposedly so friendly, that a couple of times we found tourists coming onto our back deck, unannounced and uninvited - they believed our yacht was a tourist attraction. My husband always asked them, *How would you like it if I went to your house and invited myself into your backyard?!* Most apologized and got off, but it was unsettling when we came home from getting groceries or walking the pug to find strangers sitting on our deck. We were situated right next to the float houses, which was awesome. I made friends with a girl who lived in one, and she took great pride in showing me the renovations she was doing to it. It was beautiful. Janice told me the tourists were just as bad with the float houses. They peered into her windows, and one day, she had enough. Going to one of her double-sided pane windows, she saw a man approach and she blurted out, *Mirror, Mirror on the wall, who's the fairest of them all?* She laughed as she told me that he jumped back so fast, he almost fell off the dock. We experienced a certain camaraderie amongst those who lived on the docks. We always had someone there in case of an emergency, and great friendships were created.

It was a nice dock if you enjoyed the sound of the Coho ferry and seaplanes. I would not say it was quiet, although I liked the sound of the Coho, which runs from the USA to Canada and back daily. The horn in the fog was mystical, and one foggy morning as I sat on our back deck having an early morning coffee, I heard the foghorn and spotted a seal playing off a rock in the distance. My heart filled with amazement at the sheer majestic beauty this scene produced.

My children actually enjoyed visiting more often as it was easy for them to walk aboard a BC ferry, and we picked them up in Sidney. My oldest daughter and grandchildren loved exploring Victoria with me, visiting tourist attractions like the little train exhibition and a boating museum. My love of history was evident as I explored the many buildings and gardens within the city, sometimes alone and sometimes with my children. Even though they were young, they had a ball. One time my oldest son came and took me out for Mother's Day, which I particularly appreciated because he was also inflicted with seasickness and could not be on the yacht, even while docked.

Easter saw my second oldest and youngest daughters come for the holiday. We did a lot of touristy things and went out for Easter dinner. Of course, we also had an egg hunt and brunch. While wishing for a caramel apple with fuzzy peaches on it this past Easter, my daughter reminded me what I used to tell them:

Getting older is inevitable,
but acting your age is a matter of personal preference.

One Christmas, we decided to take Mirage down to Pender Island. We got all our supplies on board, thinking we would leave just after noon on December 23rd. Drew listened to the Coast Guard's weather report, stating that a storm was coming in late the next afternoon, so we decided to change our departure time and leave early in the morning. It was a particularly cloudy day and cold on the water. We stopped at the harbour's fuel dock and filled up with diesel, otherwise known to boaters as gold . The wind came up and was howling just as we got out into the open waters. We figured it would calm down soon because the storm was predicted for late afternoon, and it was still early morning. We may have turned around had we only known that this was the beginning of the trip from hell.

However, we were both eager to keep going. About an hour out, the swells became enormous, burying our bow five times. I was hysterical, thinking we were going to die. Charlie hid behind me, shaking the whole way. I begged Drew to turn towards the shore, and he told me that he couldn't because if we went towards the shore, we would crash against the rocks. He was the Captain, so as the terrified first mate, I hung on and didn't say anything as we went further and further out to sea. I asked him if he was frightened, and all he said was, *Well, I am a bit concerned*. Instinctively, I knew that meant we were in trouble.

It seemed like forever, but we finally hit a channel with calmer waters. It was still lumpy, but it felt like a peaceful breeze compared to what we had been through. Being out on Mirage at the mercy of the ocean gave me a perspective of how little control one has over the elements.

After another hour, we cruised into the marina at Poets Cove, a resort on Pender Island. We radioed ahead to get our slip, and one of the dockhands met us as we approached the dock. She informed us that we would be the only guests as all the other boats had cancelled. Yes, we were the only ones, I can say, daring enough to make the journey. That is one way to put it. Drew continued speaking with the girl at the dock, and I went down into the cabin, where I let out an ungodly scream. Drew heard me and yelled down to me, *What's wrong? Is the wine okay?* At which I replied, *There are eggs all over the cabin floor!* The floor was carpeted, so it was an unimaginable mess. Lesson learned from then on to ensure that our refrigerator was safely secure before leaving the port. Incredibly, the wine survived because it was tightly secured. Guess we had our priorities straight.

The resort itself is beautiful, with a hot tub, spa, and first-class restaurants. Because Drew's birthday was just a few days away, I purchased a massage for him. He went off to the spa the next day, but very tenaciously as he had never had the experience of a massage before. When he came back, I asked him how it had gone. He said, *I wanted to bring the young lady home with us.*

On Christmas morning, we awoke to snow falling. It was just perfect. Drew walked Charlie, and when he came back, we opened our gifts, phoned the children and our parents and decided to go to lunch. I felt at peace, going for short hikes, exploring the area on this quiet day. It was also comforting to simply relax on our boat. I previously made dinner reservations at the main restaurant at the resort, so off we went; it was a spectacular meal. Our table was right in front of the fireplace, and I felt very pampered.

We met the chef's girlfriend and her friend, and they came back to the boat for a nightcap. All in all, it was a magical Christmas in its own way. It was the first time I did not have 20 people at my dining table. Did I miss that? Well, let's just say I was well rested, but I missed my family terribly. Our trip back was calm, finishing our trip off with New Year's Eve on Salt Spring Island tied up at a marina. We met the owners, and we invited them down for drinks that evening. During the day,

I shopped in the little boutique stores, went for walks, and did some grocery shopping. Coffee on Salt Spring is so delicious. To anyone who goes there, I recommend visiting the coffee shop and taking some liquid gold home!

Shortly after we arrived back in Victoria, we decided to go up island again. The moorage rates had doubled in Victoria Harbour, and parking rates for our car were extremely expensive. As we did not have any real ties to Victoria, it was an easy choice to return to Campbell River. I missed our home dock and my friends.

Having our home at sea was wonderful. Along with some other necessities, all we had to do was get our groceries and wine on board and then set sail. We journeyed out to our playground in Desolation Sound all summer long, which I loved because it is steeped in history. Captain George Vancouver discovered and named it. He initially viewed it in the winter when the rain and lack of civilization made for a dreary sight – thus, the name Desolation Sound. Years later, it was to become identified as a major logging industry. This brought civilization into the area with families who worked and lived in the logging camps. Being a history buff, I ate all this information up.

We loved to anchor out under the stars as far away from the other boats as possible. During the day, we drank wine and ate from our charcuterie board on our back deck. When the sun got hot, we jumped in the water: jump in, drink wine, eat cheese, repeat! We often played Bob Marley tunes on the stereo system. In the evening, we switched it up a bit; Drew cooked on the BBQ, and when it got dark, we listened to Glenn Campbell and danced under the stars like no one was watching…because they weren't. I do miss our *Glen Campbell nights*.

We knew where the warm, clean water was, and we had

favourite spots like Pendrell Sound, Von Donup Marine Park, and Squirrel Cove. Even now, thinking back to our time spent at these places, my heart swells with joy. Penderel Sound's water can reach 80 degrees Fahrenheit in the summer and is the blueish green colour of the Caribbean. Von Donup was a quiet spot if you stayed out of the inner bay where more people congregated. The water was clean except for the white jellyfish, and we were often fortunate to see deer, bears, and wolves on the shore. There was a hiking trail, but due to the presence of wolves, we never took that road with our pup. The pug thought the dinghy was his boat, and the moment Drew began to untie it from the back of Mirage, Charlie got all excited, anticipating riding in her and almost fell in several times. He was so funny.

We hold dear Roscoe Bay, which had a freshwater lake nearby close to our hearts. It was the first spot where I actually heard a tree fall in the forest.

***It was so loud that the man in a boat anchored near us sang out, "When a tree falls in the forest…"
And I sang back, "Does anybody hear?"***

Drew looked at me and just shook his head and sighed. We could anchor out in the bay and then cruise in our dinghy to get to Black Lake. It was the site of a logging camp. When we later upsized our boat, we found it harder to anchor in the bay, and it had become a very popular place. We tried to teach Charlie how to swim in the lake, even though he didn't swim in the ocean. He sunk like a rock, so we gave up and were extremely careful around the water with him, giving him a life jacket. It was a good thing because years later, he accidentally fell off the wharf in Campbell River, and the little so and so frantically doggie paddled to get to shore. He was too stubborn for words, not even wanting to try to swim.

For the most part, we avoided the resorts, only stopping to buy gas or water. However, there were a few we loved, with our first choice being Gorge Harbour. There were times when we headed in there for a few nights on our way to Von Donup. This resort included a swimming pool, laundry facilities, a grocery store, a beautiful restaurant, and a boat dock where we could get gas or diesel fill-ups. As most boaters know, making friends with other boaters is easy. Many are just as laid back and out looking for a relaxing adventure. We had couples off million-dollar yachts stopping by for a cocktail or two, as well as a few younger people on skiffs. There's a saying, *When you are on the water, the sun always shines*. Entering Gorge Harbour, there are views of the pictographs on the cliffs created by the Indigenous bands long ago. Drew and I took our dinghy over to Manson's Landing that held a village with a dance hall and post office. I delighted in the large tidal pools and swimming off the white sandy beach.

We actually met Arnold Schwarzenegger. It was a nice summer afternoon, and we were anchored at Rebecca Spit on Quadra Island. We noticed a big yacht behind us in deeper water, and a man in his dinghy came up. We chatted with him for quite a while, both thinking it was Arnold we were having a conversation with due to his accent. Wanting to preserve his privacy, we didn't ask. We weren't certain of his identity until he took off back to his yacht, waving at us and yelling, *Hosta la vista baby*. All three of us laughed.

Boating trips and my love of learning about the past held their own magic, and after a time, I became most excited and full of joy while on the water, heading to all the places we visited. I would never have imagined living on a boat before I met Drew;

it was mind-boggling. I ate up as much of each community's historical identity as I constantly read about the locals and the ancestral community roots. I found myself reading about the people and places before we arrived, and I was always on the lookout for evidence of prior life and what they experienced long ago. It was fascinating to me.

Refuge Cove was one of our frequent haunts. The docks are small, so we did not attempt moorage with our larger boat, Mirage. However, we did make the voyage on the 27-foot boat Drew owned when I met him. The area is a rustic co-op type of existence lying on the territorial lands of the Klahoose people. The Cove was settled in the early 1900s by the Black, McGuffie and Smith families. They hunted and logged the land to make ends meet. Several of the cabins on site are still in use today. Refuge Cove itself has an all-in-one grocery store, post office, and liquor store, along with a coffee kiosk and book exchange. These are all owned and run by those who live in the co-op. I will never forget my first purchase of coffee at the establishment, asking, *What kind of coffee do you have?* A man with a gruff voice answered very curtly, *What do you think this is, Tim Hortons?* I never asked again.

Lund is the Mosquito capital of the world. That is why we always took our youngest daughter with us as she attracted the bugs, and they left us alone. Oops, just kidding - I will be in trouble for that one!! Lund was originally settled by the Thulin brothers in 1889, coming from Sweden. They first spent the summer in Pendrell Sound, hand-logging before settling down just south of the Copeland Islands on the site of an old Indigenous village; they built a hotel on the site and named this spot Lund as it was easy to spell. Mail and supplies arrived by tugboat every three to four days. The hotel is still there today, no doubt having had several years of renovations. There is a hot

Island life

tub, a fabulous restaurant, a bar, and showers for boaters who do not have one on board. There is also a fully stocked grocery and liquor store attached to the hotel and an art gallery and bakery shop with Nancy's famous sticky buns. People sailed into the docks just for these heavenly treats. These were a must to start off our mornings off along with a warm cup of coffee while watching the sunrise, sitting on the back deck of Mirage. I truly savoured my sticky bun there and believed anything was possible.

Without a doubt, one of our trips took us as close to paradise as we could get. Drew and I made the voyage to the Princess Louisa Inlet over a period of four days. It's a long way from Campbell River, being 55 miles by boat up the Jervis Inlet. Our first stop was in Lund, and we were able to moor on the outside docks. We then went on to Skookumchuck, filling Mirage up with gas and stocking up with water for the next leg of our trip. However, as we found out later, the water wasn't drinkable. Oh well, we had vodka and wine! It was a cold and rainy ride up the Jervis channel, and I had no idea where we were going; I only knew that Drew wanted to go there, and it was a one-time deal. We had a deadline to get to the head of Princess Louisa at slack tide, otherwise we would not make it through the Malibu Rapids. With no other feasible possibilities to hang our anchor off, we sped along with the rain beating down so hard it came in the side windows.

The Inlet itself was settled in 1927 by James MacDonald, otherwise known as Mac. He managed to build a cabin made entircly of logs. Chatterbox Falls provided him with a source of energy, allowing him the comforts of home. As we headed to the entrance of Princess Louisa, we noted a camp of sorts to the left of the rapids. In 1930, Mac built a resort here to service elite yacht owners at the entrance of the inlet just inside the rapids. It was not sustainable due to World War II, but Youth for Life purchased the resort in 1954, and it became a non-denominational summer camp for teenagers. Mac often paid a visit to the camp and told stories about the area. His cabin eventually burned down, and he moved and dedicated the area to the boating community of the Pacific North West, saying, *I feel I am completing a trust.* Princess Louisa international Society teamed up with BC Parks in 1964 to maintain and preserve the integrity and beauty of the land.

Drew and I anchored out across from a former campground where a huge firepit and several outbuildings had been built. We travelled by our dingy to the head of the Inlet, where Chatterbox Falls is located. The water is very cold coming off the melting glaciers and snowcaps above, so we did not go swimming. But it was here that I experienced the overwhelming illustriousness of nature with the sound of rushing water and the magnificent spray off the rocks. Being early September, there were few visiting boats, so it was remarkably beautiful and serene at the same time. We stayed a few days, just taking in the calm and awe-inspiring scenery.

Drew and I have many memories of nature only visible on the ocean. We had a mother killer whale with her cub swim under us on our way to the Minstrel Islands and viewed dolphins dancing off the shores north of Campbell River. One summer day, on the way to Von Donup, we encountered a huge humpback whale. We turned off our engine and watched it play behind the boat. That was a bit concerning as the size of this grand creature could flip our boat. However, I guess he just wanted to entertain us because he left after a short while. We took our daughter and her friends to Middlenatch Island, where we viewed the sea lions and seals basking in the sun on the rocks.

Island life

I feel incredibly blessed to have had the opportunity to coexist with nature in all its glorious splendour. I was happiest on the water and would love to do it all over again.

It was not always fun and games living onboard. There were chores to be done regardless of the weather, and we had to take advantage of utilities when moored. The water tank had to be filled every day. You could not make a piece of toast while the heat was turned on because there wasn't enough power to accommodate both. And we were constantly at odds with the weather. There was no garbage pick-up at the docks, so we hauled our refuse up to a dumpster situated off the dock site. I once hit a man on the head while throwing my garbage bag in the dumpster; he was dumpster diving and started yelling at me. I felt terrible and quietly and kindly said, *Oops, I'm sorry.* Our washer used a ton of water and our dryer a significant amount of energy, so we barely used them, instead opting to use each harbour's laundromat.

Repairs to a boat are expensive. The saying used by boaters, *Bring on Another Thousand* is not far from the truth. Every spring, we needed to haul our boat out to a shipyard to have the bottom power washed, and because we lived on ours, this required booking a hotel for a few days. None of this was cheap. Being a heavy-duty mechanic, my husband could do most of the repairs himself, but the parts cost a lot of money. Even regular maintenance was not inexpensive, and it always seemed there was something to repair. We sold our yacht in 2014 and moved from Vancouver Island to the Okanagan.

Would I trade this experience in for a land-loving one? I would not! However, the Universe shifted my world, and I am grateful for the chance to have lived with the love of my life on our beautiful Mirage.

Mirage, my home for five and a half years,
is shown here anchored out in Walsh Cove.
I learned how to live simply day to day
with gratitude and respect...
respect for the history of the land and gratitude for the
opportunity to live amongst the sea life we encountered
while cruising the Pacific coast.

VIII

Finding Paradise

After everything I had gone through in the past, I thought my life was on the upswing, having met and married Drew and experiencing a peaceful life on our boat for a few years. But in 2010, the universe had another plan, presenting great adversity amidst blessings with the passing of my son, Nicholas. We decided to move to the mainland, and the impact of selling Mirage was still bittersweet. I missed spending time on our boat, but it was time to move forward, and new adventures awaited us. Little did I know how much of an adventure I was in for as I yearned for the inner peace I found in a little piece of paradise.

After we sold our yacht, Drew wanted to try living in the Okanagan of British Columbia. Drew and I were in the backyard of our house on Vancouver Island, enjoying a couple of glasses of wine. We were about to go inside when Drew turned to me and asked, *Do you want to live in the Okanagan?* What on earth had this man planned now? He said we would be closer to our daughter, who lived in the West Kootenays and was having a baby very soon. I replied, *Sure, okay,* and went off to bed thinking it was the wine talking. We had discussed purchasing a home previous to this, but there was never any mention of moving off the rock. Because Drew worked just outside of the Alaskan border, we could move anywhere with an airport close by.

The next morning after breakfast, he sat down at our

computer and started looking at homes for rent in Osoyoos. I had never been to Osoyoos, so I thought it was near my daughter's house. I came to find out it was a four-hour drive from her. He saw a couple of condominiums for rent in a complex on the beach and decided he would give one of the owners a call. I still thought he was just investigating the possibility. The man he spoke with said he was an airline pilot who only used the place in the summer, and we could rent it from September to June. Because it was a four-bedroom townhouse, it would allow us to have more of our children gather at our home, so I considered this a good idea. Once again, I thought Drew made a good point, indicating that it was not as far for our children to travel to us with no ferry involved. It was not a long-term commitment, and if I changed my mind, we could just move back to the island. So, I agreed -another day and another plot twist. Off we went.

This time, we packed up all our belongings, moved away from the ocean and lived in a home on a lake. It pleased me that the townhouse was on the water's edge and came with a heated community swimming pool and private beach. I felt we needed both because Osoyoos is in the desert with summer temperatures soaring from the high 30s in the summer to not much change at night. When our lease ended, we had yet to decide where we wanted to put down our roots, so we rented another unit overlooking the swimming pool in the same development.

I had fallen ill, so I thought it was a good idea to postpone house-hunting until I felt better. At this point, I had a nurse coming weekly to help me with my diabetic wounds and an organization called Better at Home providing biweekly housekeeping while Drew was away in camp. It was an interesting rental on the top floor of a duplex. A man lived below us who literally thought he was God. He should never have lived below another family, and he made no bones about complaining and banging with a broom day and night on our floor, which was his ceiling. He told me not to flush the toilet at night and that when I walked around, I was too noisy. I weighed 89 pounds due to my ill health, and I was alone most of the time; go figure. Also, my mobility was compromised, so going up and down the stairs to answer the door was difficult. I tried to feel compassion for his need for quiet. However, besides learning to levitate, I could not be quiet enough in his eyes, so we could not reach a mutual win-win. I finally told him every time he complained that he should move to a place where he did not live below another unit. I thought if I told him enough times, the message would get through, but it didn't because he continued to harass me. He was a border security agent, and I think he believed he could order anyone around, including me. He seemed to be in his ego a lot and wasn't used to the kind of feedback I gave him. But I decided that I wouldn't play nice in the sandbox with someone who disrespected me the way he did.

    One night, my daughter, son-in-law, and baby were visiting. We had our dinner, and because I was still recovering, I made for my bed almost immediately after. My son-in-law proceeded to lay down with my baby granddaughter, and suddenly my daughter came into my room and asked if I was banging on the wall. I told her no, so she checked on her husband and baby and found them almost asleep. We had spoken about our neighbour below and his harassment, so she put two and two together. She immediately burst down the stairs and began banging on his door with great force. He opened the door, and she got right in his face and yelled *How dare you do this to my mother!! She is not well!* He was caught off guard and answered,

I Almost Lost My Marbles…Until I Didn't

Well, she is so noisy! My daughter warned him that if he did not stop, she would be back. Bravo to my daughter! I have never been prouder of her, sounding like Arnold in the Terminator.

The next thing we knew, the property manager came over as he had witnessed what was going on. He said laughingly, *I come in peace.* We were all awake at this point, and he asked what happened. He encouraged us to make a formal complaint to the strata as this person was also renting his suite, and this was not the first time he had pestered others who rented the unit we were in.

My children loved visiting Osoyoos. My youngest son has a friend whose parents own an RV, and they rented a spot on Osoyoos Lake at Nk'Mip winery. My son came often and usually brought guests. They enjoyed boating and bonfire parties late at night, and I enjoyed their company. My daughters equally loved the wineries in and around Osoyoos, and we enjoyed many wine tasting tours together within the town limits, along with many more not far away in Oliver. I made it a habit to visit the Nk'Mip winery as well. It offers a golf club, where my two youngest enjoyed many rounds of golf, wine tours, and hiking trails, as well as an excellent restaurant. There are also many fruits and vegetable stands offering the fresh taste of produce I love such as tomatoes, beans, cherries, peaches, and apples from the local orchards. An added perk is Osoyoos Lake, where I loved swimming. It is the warmest lake in Canada, making the town a very popular tourist destination. Summertime was booming, however the winters were long and dreary. There was definitely a lack of good doctors, and the nearest hospital was almost an hour away. Due to my health concerns, these factors led us to look elsewhere when we were ready to purchase our forever home.

It seemed a natural progression to move to Peachland,

a town just southwest of Kelowna, BC. Drew and I took frequent road trips there, and driving along the road beside Okanagan Lake filled a piece of our hearts that had been missing in Osoyoos. We often had lunch at a local restaurant which quickly became our favourite. The weather was a tad more moderate, and the access to good doctors was important to me. Along with the proximity to the Kelowna General Hospital, the move was a no-brainer. But I had to be certain, so we checked out surrounding areas such as Summerland, Penticton and Kelowna, and it took us over a year to rule out many different options – we always came back to Peachland.

***It seemed my heart was drawn to the history
and lake-life this small town had to offer.***

We purchased our one-level townhouse with an unobstructed view of Okanagan Lake and Okanagan Mountain in November of 2016. The house is smaller than I would have liked, but unless we have the children visiting, it's usually just myself until Drew comes home from working away. Drew and I and our children, who visit often, have spent many nights on our deck watching the moon over the lake and the mountain while enjoying a good bottle of local wine. They love Drew, and his love for them is evident. He truly loves all my children as his own, along with our three grandchildren. This makes me love him all the more.

Our complex is situated high on a mountainside, so we are graced with wonderful wildlife that visit us regularly. I have been fortunate to spot a white-tailed deer, a moose, a mother bear and her cub, a wolf, and a cougar off our deck. One night, I awoke to a loud roar outside our bedroom window. Drew was sound asleep, and although it sounded like a huge dog, I could not be sure what animal was causing the noise. I looked outside, and this large animal was looking at the house with its great big glowing eyes. I tried to wake Drew up, but once asleep, that man is out like a light. All he mumbled was that coyotes are in the hills. Not making much sense, he fell back asleep. The next day, our neighbour mentioned that he had also seen the coyote; being kind of clueless sometimes, I asked how it got through the gate. Drew was quick to say maybe someone gave him the code. Duh, I suppose he *could* have just climbed down the embankment beside the mailboxes.

I enjoy sitting on our deck watching the eagles fly by in the summertime. They soar and dance in the sky, making my spirit come alive in such a wonder-filled way.

> *When my son passed away, I told him,*
> *Nicholas, soar with the eagles,*
> *and I often feel his presence with me as*
> *I watch these majestic birds in flight.*

My hummingbird feeder is a hub of activity during the spring and early summer. From my viewpoint, we can watch the array of boats on the water; the sailboats, pontoon boats, party boats, and jet skis. It has become a family tradition to rent a pontoon boat once a year and go out on the lake with our children, always having tons of fun. I usually get submarine sandwiches for our picnic lunch, and out we go with Captain Drew. He always stops the boat long enough for us to jump in the water for a swim and then eat our lunch.

Peachland is steeped in a historical past. So, of course, this is right up my alley. Many of the old buildings have been preserved and repurposed. After talking to some of the older members of the town I was told the town was founded by John Moore

Robinson who was a mining prospector and land developer in 1909. Originally named Camp Hewitt, the town was officially incorporated and named Peachland after the delicious tasting peaches in the area. Robinson also founded Summerland and Naramata under his company name, The Peachland Township Company. It has a deep history in the logging, mining, and fur trade. Local farmers provided provisions for the miners, and this is how the founder came across the peaches. There is also a public hiking trail leading to the old goldmine entrance. I have never taken it, but those who have tell me it is like stepping back in time. I often wonder what life would have been like back in the pioneer days.

The town boasts a museum based in a historic eight-sided Baptist church, dating back to 1909 that I love to visit frequently. There is an old one-room schoolhouse in town that is still intact and lends itself out to groups such as artists and yogis who teach classes there. The main street is Beach Avenue, running parallel to the Okanagan lakefront. Along this street is a second schoolhouse, which now holds the town's art gallery and visitor center. A sushi restaurant now replaces an original laundry service. There is an elementary school here, but high school-aged children are bussed into West Kelowna. To me, this town's connection to the past is heart-warming, and my mind often wanders back in time to when a steamboat was the only way to travel to Kelowna. I can imagine going down to the docks in the morning, riding on the lake, and then setting foot on the other side to pick up supplies. It was a simpler time without the amenities of today, with some commuters actually driving on the ice when the lake froze over. A bridge now connects all surrounding communities to Kelowna.

There is a pub just down the street a little further. It was originally called the Lakeview Hotel and had a feed store below it. It then became known as the Edgewater Inn, which was home to the founder of Peachland at one time. In the 1950s, the name changed with a new owner to the Totem Pole Inn, now a busy bar with live weekend entertainment. Pete Spackman bought it and carved a totem pole in the front yard beside the street. On the top of the totem pole was a carving of the Ogopogo, the resident lake monster whose home lies on Rattlesnake Island across the lake from Peachland. Today it is a bustling bar where locals and tourists alike gather to enjoy drinks and be entertained by live music on the weekends. It has been renamed by the new owner as The Edgewater Bar and Grill.

I can see the Island from our deck view, and this legend has captivated my imagination since we moved here. The Interior Salish First Nation first spoke about the Ogopogo as N'xaxaitk (syilx/ok), or the devil spirit of the lake. Some historians tell of a Metis settler in 1855 who crossed the lake in a canoe, pulling a team of horses when the Ogopogo approached. The horses dipped down into the lake, and he had to cut the ropes so the canoe would not capsize. Susan Allison, who was the first non-native settler to see the monster in 1872, stated that it appeared as a dinosaur in the water. She was one of the first Europeans to reach out and develop communication with the Okanagan Indigenous Band. Her homestead was where Quails Gate winery is now situated. I can only imagine what it would have been like to capture a peek at the Ogopogo swimming out in the waters just off the shore.

Sightings persist even as late as last year. Different tales refer to the Ogopogo as a sturgeon over 100 years old. Others believe he is an aquatic serpent from prehistoric times. Whatever he is, the economy has benefited from this seemingly harmless creature from the unknown. Everyone agrees on one thing - the Ogopogo presents itself with a mysterious big wave even in calm waters. Our granddaughter keeps a close eye out for him when she visits but has yet to see the monster through Grandpa Drew's binoculars. I find the history of this region fascinating.

Rattlesnake Island has a very interesting history all its own. It was originally called Sunset Island and privately owned by Pete Spackman. But in 1970, Eddy Haymour bought the piece of land and renamed it Ogopogo Island. Haymour intended to turn it into an Arabian theme park with rides, mini-golf, restaurants, a castle, and a giant camel. Unfortunately, he had many issues with local and provincial authorities over sewage disposal, boat docking safety, and public health. He became so enraged with the government that he threatened them and was sentenced to time in jail and then to a psychiatric hospital in 1973. He was released in 1975 and returned to his homeland of Lebanon.

With the aid of some of his relatives, he held hostages at the Canadian embassy there. He then returned to Canada and sued the Canadian government. The result was the Canadian government reviewing his case and paying him 250,000 dollars. The BC government then took over the island as a protected parkland and named it Rattlesnake Island. Remnants of the theme park remain, including parts of the mini golf course, and anyone touring the island by boat can stop and get off to visit. However, this may not be the best place to disembark for those with a fear of snakes. Haymour went on to purchase a home along Highway 97 west of Peachland, turning it into an Airbnb that still stands today.

Moving along Peachland's Beach Avenue is the Sunnyside Market. I learned this was once a general store run by Len and Ken Faulks, who are direct decedents of the famous explorer James Cook. The building originally held J.R. Robinson's real estate office on the top floor and a convenience store on the lower level.

Every summer from May to September there is a farmer's market in Heritage Park where I love to browse the stands, finding local produce, as well as crafts and homemade products from honey and jams to candles and jewelry. The park holds a children's playground where I take my youngest granddaughter when she comes to visit. This summer, a splash park is being built, and I am so excited to take her there. There is also a newly built pier with wheelchair accessibility and areas to fish for the mobility challenged. I value the respect our community has for diversity.

There is a rainbow sidewalk painted in front of the art gallery – the inclusivity and welcoming of all ages, genders, and abilities of people warms my heart.

There are two marinas. One allows for the rental of boats, and another is private for the yacht club. The main swimming area is aptly named Swim Bay and boasts the only lifeguard on Lake Okanagan. It is very popular in the summer and has rafts, swing ropes, and diving boards. It also has a wheelchair-accessible water entry that Rick Hansen designed intended to make swimming available for all. Lastly, it has a concession stand, selling fast food such as hot dogs, fish and chips, pop, and ice cream.

Drew, our children and I opt for the other less crowded spots in the busy summer months. It is well known that if you want to use any of the other beaches, you need to stake your spot by nine in the morning. Many of them have picnic tables, and Drew and I are often relegated to finding and securing the location. We are old as dirt, so we are up early and let the younger ones sleep in. We are proud to call our oldest daughter *Peachland Bum Bum* because she would live at the beach all day, every day if she could. The water in Lake Okanagan is cooler than Osoyoos Lake, but last year, it reached a warm 23 degrees Celsius, so we enjoyed swimming even more. I have seen water skiers and kayakers on the lake as early as mid-April, and in August there is a swim event to cross the lake over to Rattlesnake Island and back; kayakers accompany the swimmers as spotters. When the season shifts to winter, there is, of course, the infamous annual polar bear swim.

My youngest brings all the fun stuff to the beach, such as a floating island, a kayak, and tubes that we all take pleasure in. My second oldest daughter recently moved to Kelowna, and I am very excited to have one of my children living close to me. She and I love taking her dog to the doggie beach just down from our home.

I have had many meals in the wonderful restaurants along the strip in this beautiful town I live in, including a wide variety of cuisine from Italian, German, Japanese, Asian fusion, as well as fish and chips and pizza. Drew and I tend to eat out more in the winter because it's easier to make a reservation, but the restaurant patios are a wonderful place to sip a glass of wine and look over the lake on a hot summer day. In the spring, the World Classic Car Show draws hundreds of participants and spectators. A local realtor provides a shuttle bus to the downtown area as parking is a premium due to the number of classic cars on display up and down the roads. Because of his generosity and given my mobility issues, I can attend this event as it makes walking much more doable. Unfortunately, it was cancelled in 2020 due to Covid-19; however, it usually attracts thousands of viewers. There is live music, and the Blues Brothers perform in their *police car*. Last time I was there, I sat on a bench overlooking the water while a band took me back to my past, playing Janis Joplin and Credence Clearwater Revival. I had the time of my life.

Tourists book Airbnb's or one of the many bed and breakfast rentals that continued to be popular even throughout the pandemic. There is also an RV park, but it is sadly up for sale. Our children prefer to pile themselves into our home as the price is right. We only have one extra bedroom, so Bring Your Own Bed brings new meaning to BYOB.

The lure of Peachland in itself is enough for me, but it also provides close proximity to many of the different local wineries and distilleries. Just as in Osoyoos, Drew and I enjoy the fresh fruit and vegetables from many fruit stands along the highway. The peaches, cherries, apples, and pears are all from the local orchards and a delightful addition to any meal. In addition, we are able to grow on our back deck tomatoes dill and chives.

A short distance down from Peachland is the Kettle Valley Railway which operates during the summer months taking tourists on a train ride through the valley. I have never had an opportunity to participate in this attraction, but it is on my bucket list. There is also a zip line for those who are more adventurous than me.

Some of our small town traditions had to change due to restrictions during Covid, but once again, our community rose to the occasion by not cancelling events, instead having them take on a different look. For example, on Halloween, the Boys and Girls Club usually hosts a party for the youth in Peachland. This could not be done safely during the pandemic, so our community decorated the pier with pumpkins and pots of candy. The children were able to social distance and walk along the boardwalk to gather the treats. In the evening, cars went through the neighbourhoods blasting ghoulish music and throwing candy into the children's hands who waited on their front lawns. Many parents commented they would love these traditions to carry on post-pandemic.

I appreciate and love the creativity of the community-minded people who make up this town. We have a senior's home that is fairly new and is rent to income for any senior over 55. Unfortunately for many, there is a fairly long waiting list.

The Peachland Wellness Center located downtown has been a godsend to me. It is an organization made up of primarily volunteers and is funded partially through the United Way and private donations. It provides rides through volunteer drivers to essential appointments like going to the doctor, the bank, or the grocery store. Some drivers even pick up groceries for those who are unable or feel at risk to go to the store themselves. Many of their programs, such as light housekeeping, are provided free of charge to those who require these services because they are no longer able to manage them independently. Social programs like Friendly Visitors, singing, card playing, and coffee clubs are also offered for free. During Covid restrictions, the Wellness Center could not host a Christmas dinner at the 50-Plus Club. This dinner is highly anticipated every year by those of all ages who would otherwise be alone on Christmas day or may not be able to prepare their turkey dinner due to financial or physical limitations. Once again, several generous volunteers thought outside of the box and helped prepare dinners while others drove around distributing them, along with a wee gift. Like so many other traditions, the annual tree-lighting was done by zoom.

We have beautiful boutique-like stores, gift and coffee shops, and a library here in Peachland, along with essential offerings like a grocery store, two pharmacies, a post office, and a dental office. There is also a thrift shop, hardware store, and even a business providing kayak and paddleboard rentals. We are so fortunate to have an abundance of health care services, including a spa for acupuncture and massage therapy. Peachland gives me all I love and require, and I can take a taxi or call for a volunteer driver to drive me anywhere when Drew is away, including down to the beach. As I sit on a bench, gazing out on the water, I feel so blessed with the nature and history that surrounds me and fills my soul. This is truly my happy place.

Living in the Okanagan feeds my creative spirit. When I feel the imbalance from everyday stress, walking on the beach boardwalk with my hubby helps me relax and find clarity. The locals refer to our small town as a little piece of paradise. And this is true for Drew and me.

Finding Paradise

The beach in Peachland, our forever home.
This is defiantly my happy place.
I am able to find peace and calm even within
all the chaos the world.
The waves gently crashing upon the shore bring me
into a space I can regenerate and renew.

IX

Chronic Illness Will Never Define me

In what seemed to be the blink of an eye, life changed for me in 2014 when I was diagnosed with several chronic illnesses, one by one with diabetes, chronic obstructive pulmonary disease, low kidney function, and congestive heart failure. I have also survived cancer twice. I'm learning to live with the new restrictions that come hand-in-hand with these illnesses and have begun the journey of accepting my new challenges. I am discovering what balance and connection are for me and how to live my best life in a new way.

I have grieved my old life, but part of me did not want to let go of who I used to be. I kicked at the dirt, hoping I would get better, but realizing at the same time that this is now my reality. I found myself manifesting, saying, *I can do this, I will get better* over and over again. I hoped I could reverse my conditions and finally accepted that, for now, this is the new me. It is one I had not bargained for, but here I am, learning to live with illnesses that seek to define me. This is not easy.

I find comfort in helping friends I made on social media going through any or all of my illnesses. This is where I can be me, authentically. On the inside, I am the same person I was 15 years ago. I still love unconditionally, have empathy and respect for others, and prioritize using my ability to make people laugh. These are the values that keep me moving forward and quiet my thoughts back to a feeling of calm. The most important thing I can do in my life is to help make the world a calmer, more joyful place one person at a time.

Early one winter morning, while preparing to fly to my daughter's home in Vancouver for Christmas, I realized the blisters on my ankles had become worse and quite painful. I first noticed them several months ago but avoided going to the doctor; I felt less worried about being in denial than facing the inevitable, so this is where I chose to be. In hindsight, this was not one of my better plans. We had moved to Osoyoos that September and did not have a doctor yet, so even though I was slightly concerned, I hid my fears and ankles from Drew, along with many odd things that were happening to my body. I used to enjoy white wine, and, ironically, having just moved to Wine Country, I was sick to my stomach after drinking one glass. It was strange, but what's a girl to do? I switched to red but found my system didn't tolerate it either. I then became constantly thirsty, starting my day off with apple juice, moving on to lunch with iced tea, and finishing with a glass of wine in the evening.

My daughter's sister-in-law, Michelle, and a family friend wanted to get together for a Christmas drink before we flew out. So, after pouring her a glass of wine and a rum and eggnog for me, she happened to see my ankles and asked, *Honey, are your ankles sore?* I admitted they were. After a bit of convincing, she took me to the hospital in Oliver to get something for the pain. When we arrived, she and I were ushered into a patient room in the ER, where they called in a doctor to see my blisters. Michelle kept taking pictures, which I thought was odd. She told me she was sending the images to her boss to explain why she needed the next day off. She said, I want to be the one to drive you to the airport. Unbeknownst to me, she sent them to my oldest daughter to alert her to what was going on. The nurse came in and asked if I was diabetic. I told her I wasn't, but my husband is. She then pricked my finger to check my sugars.

The nurse looked shocked, telling me the glucose number was at 27. Michelle asked, *Out of what?* I didn't know much more than she did but I had a feeling I had failed the test. The nurse simply looked at me, shook her head and answered, *I don't even know how you are walking.* The funny thing is that I didn't feel unwell.

Then, the doctor came back into the room and told me that normal blood sugar numbers are between five and six, and I needed to be admitted until they got my numbers down. I was having none of that. I was on my way to my daughter's for Christmas, which, in my opinion, is the single most important day of the year to be connected with my children in person. So, I signed out against the doctor's advice, and my friend took me home. I still planned on flying out the next day because my children were on the lower mainland and Drew was in camp; if I was sick, I didn't want to be stuck in the interior of BC by myself.

Upon arriving at the Vancouver airport the next day, I was met by three of my children. They asked me where I wanted to go for lunch, and I decided on Earls at the mall. It was next to Toys R Us, and I wanted to look for a gift for my youngest granddaughter. We ate our lunch, and when I went to leave the table, my oldest daughter told me that we needed to test my blood sugars before we went shopping. I told her it could wait, but they insisted. So, we went to the Richmond Hospital, where they did some tests, including blood work and then released me. By this time, I was tired and went to bed after agreeing we would all meet at the mall's restaurant in the morning before getting started on my Christmas shopping list.

Everything went smoothly until I got a call from the hospital, telling me I needed to get back there as quickly as possible. They were worried because one of the tests showed that my wounds were infected, and the infection was going into the bone. I still felt fine, but the kids were adamant I go back, so off I went. It was December 23rd, and I was to remain in the hospital until New Year's Eve. At that point, I went to my youngest daughter's home, accompanied by a heavy dose of antibiotics administered through a pic line. I stayed with her until February 6th. Drew had flown in from camp on Christmas Eve to be with me in the hospital and left to go back mid-January when I was deemed out of danger of losing my feet. This was a first, and once again, I thought I would lose my marbles when the doctor came and told me that I had skin cancer, but I was too ill with diabetic wounds to operate. Drew and I were both in a state of shock, and oddly enough, I still didn't feel sick.

The doctor indicated that I was close to losing both my feet. However he believed he used the right antibiotic, so he was hopeful. Really? Oh my! This was such a surreal experience for me as I never worried that I would ever have part of my body amputated; I never thought that was a possibility. I intended to get out of the Richmond in one piece. And then, on top of that, he was telling me I had skin cancer and wasn't sure I could withstand an operation? He told me that if and when I was well enough, he would refer me to a surgeon. I didn't panic as the shock shielded me from reality, and eventually, my wounds recovered, as did my soul. I was confident that I had diabetes beat. Yeah, right - I found out it is not that simple.

This experience took its toll on me. I became afraid to eat the wrong foods, so I simply cut way back on my meals and went from 135 pounds down to 89. It was now that I looked and felt awful. Being back in Osoyoos, one of the cashiers at the gas station told my husband how good he was to his mother, meaning me. Although I knew I looked like a skeleton, and that likely aged me, I was devastated and cried all the way home. I had no energy nor appetite. The doctor I had at the time had poor communication skills, and he bluntly told me he was sure I had pancreatic cancer. I wondered what could happen next and arranged a ride with the Better at Home organization to have a scan in Penticton that day. Drew was flying into Penticton from camp that night, so I took a hotel room. After arriving back at the hotel, I received a call from my doctor. He asked if I was sitting down, and I told him I was, dreading the worst. He told me that he couldn't believe it, but my pancreas was clear. I was so excited that I ran out of the room and hugged a member of the housekeeping staff. I was lucky she was kind and didn't slap me.

As time went on, this same doctor told me he thought I had lung cancer and, at one point, I was going to lose my feet - talk about the agent of doom. If it had not been for my community nurse, I would have been extremely afraid, but she encouraged both me and Drew not to go to a dark place. I came to know that he was this way with all his patients. Having no choice but to use him due to a shortage of doctors in the area, I kept seeing him. On the positive side, he did send me to a diabetic dietitian who advised me to eat, *Go get a doughnut. If you have high numbers, we can deal with that. We have medicine to solve the high glucose numbers, but at this rate, you are becoming undernourished.* That woke me up, and as a result, I think I may have over-compensated! I won't share what I weigh now, but I'm blaming it on the refrigerator door malfunctioning.

I still was not feeling 100 percent in 2015, but it was Christmas, and I was going to Vancouver to be with my family. I was prepared this time, so what could go wrong? I had my medication with me, watched what I ate and drank, and was determined to have fun with my children and grandchildren.

I made it through the holiday without any complications... almost. The day after Boxing Day, my two daughters went to a pub; I stayed back because I was afraid to drink. I was sitting with my granddaughter when I became very irritable. I remember watching Family Feud, and I got very grumpy with her. This was completely out of character for me, especially as my granddaughter and I have a very strong relationship. I went outside to calm down, and when I came in, I was aware that something was off. I phoned my daughter to ask her to come home and take me to the emergency department at Richmond Hospital. My feet were so swollen that I could not get my shoes on. Maybe this was when I was actually going to lose my marbles! I was admitted right away with tests on my heart: an electrocardiogram, a computerized tomography, and an ultrasound. My daughter called the camp my husband was working in and told him he needed to get there as soon as he could as I was having issues with my heart. All I could think about was here we go again!

I spent three nights in the ER as there were no beds available for me on a ward. By this time, I was so emotionally tired and fed up that I just wanted to go home. I was fearful, and no one was telling me what was going. Drew arrived the next day, and they were finally able to get me onto a ward. While being transferred from the stretcher to the bed I heard the nurse ask me to turn over and Drew's voice offering to help her. All I remember was thinking, *Not right now later, I'm too tired*. The next thing I knew, I woke up in the intensive care unit, seeing Drew crying with his face in his hands. At this point, I was confused but not afraid. A doctor came in smiling broadly and asked if I knew where I was. My sarcastic self wanted to say *Disneyland*, but I told him I was in the hospital.

Apparently, my heart and lungs filled with fluid, and I

coded. Luckily, they were able to bring me back, but the doctor indicated it was a close call. My reply was, *I guess God didn't want me;* we laughed, and Drew just shook his head. I was diagnosed with COPD, which is a lung disease. Drew still didn't think I was going to make it, and to this day he cannot remember what happened in the hospital room that night because he has it blocked out. All my children flew in from Prince Rupert, Toronto and Trail. Once again, there were no beds on the regular ward, so I couldn't leave the ICU, but I didn't mind because I was in a room overlooking the park, and it came with one-on-one nursing and a big screen TV. The doctor called me *Sunshine*, saying it was a miracle I survived. I asked how close I was to not being alive. He told me that I was in the right place at the right time... *If you believe in God, it was divine intervention. If not, you have good genes. I am just happy you made it through.* I looked him in the eye and said, *You think you are happy; me too! I'm rather stubborn like that.* He smiled, and that was enough to warm any dark thoughts I may have had.

On my third day in the hospital, my nurse asked me if I wanted to sit in the chair and eat my breakfast. I said, *Of course.* When Drew came in early that morning, he saw me sitting in that chair, and the look of absolute joy on his face is hard to describe. He said, *Who are you?* I laughed, knowing I had turned the corner and was on the road to recovery. From that day on, he and I went for walks around the ward, first with a walker and then with a cane. To be discharged, I had to pass an oxygen test and walk with my nurse for six minutes. On that fateful day, we passed a room where nurses and housekeeping staff watched and cheered me while high-fiving me. They either really liked me, or they wanted me gone. Whichever it was, their support warmed my heart. I passed the criteria and was allowed to leave. One nurse came in while I was preparing to leave and asked what I would do first when I got out. *Drink a margarita*, I said. He told me he would meet me in the park in an hour.

When I left the hospital a week after arriving, I was very weak. I had to relearn how to walk again. I started with a cane, and if I was walking a long distance, say around a mall, I had the option to use a wheelchair. Once, my grandson and I had a race around the mall. His mother kept telling us to slow down, but we were having too much fun. At the insistence of my husband, I practiced walking every chance I could; he constantly pushed me. With massage therapy and walking along our beach, I have progressed to maintaining a good stride. Sometimes, I can be a lot for Drew to handle. He has been my rock throughout all of this, never letting me give up or give in. His encouragement has and continues to be such a blessing.

Living with this medical condition inspired my commitment to keep going. I certainly have good days and not-so-good days, and I recognize them for what they are. I choose to rest on the not-so-good days and push forward on the good days. I believe I am entitled to feel sad about the loss of my health and the frustration and stress that accompanies the limited activities I can partake in. There are days I want to scream, *I just want my life back*. I usually do this to an empty wall because I keep this for when I am by myself.

As with many who suffer from any chronic illness, the loneliness I experience is not just from being alone but comes from the isolation created when friends and family do not understand.

I simply cannot participate in activities to the level I used to before my illness. I have lost friends who cannot relate. One of the contributing factors to this is the fatigue that no one fully understands unless they have been affected. There are days when my level of energy is so low that simple tasks become insurmountable. The pain in my feet and back are so debilitating at times that walking around the house is excruciating. I wake up every morning with good intentions however I have learned that when my body speaks to me, I have little choice but to listen.

Massage therapy helps my aches and pains, as does stretching, which I can do at home. There are times when I have to say no to going out as I am not up to leaving my house that day. My children accept that now as they respect that I know my limits. They, as well as my husband, encourage me to do things that make me smile and not give up. I hear from friends who suffer from chronic illness that people say they are lazy or have become anti-social. I remind them that *People who have never walked in your shoes do not understand how you feel.* For the most part, I believe people want the best for us and they think they know what that looks like. However, I have found that I am the only one who can honour myself enough to provide the boundaries I need to create.

It is especially tough when an illness is not visible to others. I do not have an oxygen tank, but I still cannot walk long distances. I do not need a wheelchair, so people question why I have an accessibility parking pass? Many surmise that I am not mobility-challenged. Recently, I surrendered my driver's license as I can no longer drive. It was an emotional event that I thought was no big deal until I signed the papers. It was like closing a chapter of my life, and I have to admit, it was harder than I thought. When I told my precious oldest daughter, she said, *There is a new chapter yet to be written, Mamma.* She always has my back.

Building a support team has never been more critical. Family and friends are an excellent source of support, but in some cases, they simply may not have the ability to understand. I consider myself lucky that my children and husband do get it. The diseases I manage will not subside over a matter of time and, as of yet, have no cure - most are progressive. Having said that, I can and choose to lead my daily life with positivity and gratitude. On the internet, there are groups where I go to chat with others experiencing the same illnesses. What has never been more important is that I look for things that provide me with joy. My daily activities may have changed, but I have tailored them to my new circumstances.

The key to managing chronic illness is to keep moving. Keeping a daily journal also helps to keep me focused and freely express my thoughts and goals for the day. I do my journaling when I get up and when it is quiet. I try to practice good eating habits as nutrition and exercise run hand in hand with managing my illnesses. Cooking meals is sometimes a challenge because the foods that are restricted on my diabetes diet are completely opposite from those on my kidney diet. For example, I should not eat nutty bread and only white for my kidneys. Yet, the carbs in white bread are not good for diabetes. I have learned the motto of *everything in moderation.* I joke with my doctor, saying, *No sugar, no salt, no carbs; please do not take away lettuce!*

I have diabetes 1.5, which is found in only ten percent of those diagnosed with diabetes and is often referred to as brittle diabetes as it is not easily managed. Normal means nothing to me, so why not? The onset of this type is usually early in life, but it often goes undiagnosed until later in life, and most often, after experiencing trauma. This makes sense for me as

Chronic Illness Will Never Define me

I became ill a couple of years after my son passed. Diabetes is a horrible disease with lows that occur when there is not enough sugar in my system, causing me to feel faint, shaky, and irritable. Short-term, these are actually more serious than high glucose numbers. I am on insulin four times a day, and if I suddenly have a low, I need to get sugar into me as soon as possible by drinking apple juice or eating chocolate to bring my numbers up.

Most of my other illnesses can be traced back to diabetes; it is why my kidney function is low and monitored to avoid kidney dialysis or a transplant. My heart problems are also attributed to diabetes, and I have diabetic wounds on my feet and arthritis in my right foot and toes. This affects my mobility, so I get to wear unappealing orthopedic shoes. If I wanted to pay this much for shoes, I would choose to buy a designer pair! My little granddaughter was here in the spring and was helping me decide what to wear. I put on my boots, and she said, *Nana are those your only shoes?* I told her they were, and she replied, *Oh, that's too bad.* Out of the mouths of babes! My fashionista was only five years old at the time.

The vascular surgeon I was seeing was convinced he was going to amputate my big toe. This was after a round of antibiotics that did not work. I went to an Interior Health Clinic every week where they treated and accessed the wound on my toe. The nurse there had the same viewpoint as the doctor. I had no intention of losing any part of my body, so I told the doctor to put me on a different antibiotic, and then we could wait to see what happens. I knew that, as a surgeon, he focused on just that - surgery. But I told him I had a plan. Then he told me, *I am the doctor, I have the plan.* I calmly looked him in the eyes and replied, *No, I have the toe, so I have the plan.* I'm guessing that no one stood up to him like that before because he looked at me kind of shocked and then laughed and, reluctantly, wrote a new prescription. It took six months, but my toe wound healed.

This same surgeon put stents in my groin to help with the circulation in my legs. We moved into our new home in Peachland within a week after I left the hospital. I received in-home nursing care and never really knew which nurse was coming on any given day. On one particular day, the nurse said she would be around about ten to ten-thirty. I wasn't familiar with this nurse, so when the doorbell rang at around ten, I answered the door to a woman I assumed was my nurse. She stood on the porch, and I said, *Hi, come on inside. I will go ahead and lie on my bed and take my pants down.* I don't know who was more surprised when she kind of blanched and replied, *I am from the Welcome Wagon.* I had a lot of explaining to do! Fortunately, my nurse arrived shortly after, validating my story. Funny, the Welcome Wagon lady never laughed and went through her presentation and left very quickly. The nurse said that's one for the books, and she and I had a good laugh.

My diseases do not define me, but instead, I continue to learn how to redefine them. I had to leave some of my old habits behind, and I needed to adjust to new limitations and adapt my daily activities. All of this has been life-altering, and I have come to realize that I can view parts of this in a positive way. I quit smoking, and my diet is better; two obvious pluses for my health, although I'm sure the stocks in potato chips soared after I quit! I cannot drive, but I never liked driving anyway. I am still able to enjoy swimming and boating just as I did before. I still love spending time with Drew and my children touring the Okanagan and wine tasting, playing at the beach with my youngest granddaughter, and hanging out with my eldest grandbabies.

Studies have shown that experiencing the death of a loved one can profoundly affect one's health, both mentally and physically. My health started to deteriorate since the death of my son. I admit I did not take care of myself during that time, increasing my smoking to three packs a day and drinking way more than I should have. I think back, and it was like my heart was breaking in pieces, so I turned to alcohol and cigarettes to ease the pain. I stuffed my feelings down with substance abuse.

As a life coach, I knew better. I saw the signs, but I was in emotional distress and ignored them. My diagnosis of COPD and diabetes prompted me to manage my drinking, and after having smoked for 45 years, I immediately stopped with the aid of nicotine patches. Being addicted to nicotine made quitting the most challenging thing I have ever done, and until the nicotine was out of my system, I had horrible nightmares. The craving nearly sent me over the moon at times, and, once again, I thought I was going to lose my marbles!! It helped that I remembered the feeling of not being able to catch a breath to keep me on track and sane. To this day, I still have the odd moment when tempted. However, I have learned that this is a habit-based reaction. The addiction to nicotine ends within the first week of stopping smoking, but the habits I associated with having a cigarette were the hardest to break, and I needed to retrain my brain.

The first thing I used to do in the morning was get up and reach for my cigarettes. Then, I had my coffee while smoking and even smoked in the car. Stopping those habits was the hard part, but I was determined because I knew the next cigarette I put to my lips could end my life.

I associated smoking with my morning coffee and when I was bored in the afternoon or lighting up after dinner. Eventually, I learned to replace these habits with different, healthier choices. What is interesting is that I can't honestly say I feel so much better because I stopped too late and deal with being short of breath even without them. I know I would be much worse if I continued smoking, but the damage was already done before I quit. It is the loss of my independence that has been the greatest adjustment; being able to get up and go without preplanning everything would be such a treat. And yet, life isn't that bad at all! I wake up in the morning with the mindset that I can do everything I want to, yet a lot of times, it is a fight just to make my breakfast. But get up, I do, and I get on with what I can.

Chronic Obstructive Pulmonary Disease, otherwise known as COPD, has been the most restrictive illness I have to date. I am considered to be in the early stages and take a puffer every morning to ease the mucus on my lungs. This is also a progressive disease. However, it can be managed with exercise, medications, and to a certain extent, diet. When I was first diagnosed, I knew nothing about COPD, so I joined an online support group and met many people from all over the world in different stages of the disease. I managed to make many good friends on this online site, and it was good for me in so many ways, finding information when I need it and receiving inspiration from others. Initially, it was very frightening, and I met many strong warriors as I moved forward with this illness. My counselling mind bounded before me as it provided me with the opportunity to support others while making a positive difference in their day as I encourage them to keep going through the good days and bad. They, in turn, also feed my need for connection, and I feel so blessed to have them in my life as they give me peace of mind and fill my heart with joy, along with a ton of support when I am in need.

COPD has many different names, with emphysema,

chronic bronchitis, and sometimes asthma under its umbrella – mine is asthma-related. At first, I had no idea what COPD stood for. I had the misperception that only people who were on oxygen had this illness. I smoked, and this was defiantly the contributing cause. However, I learned that some people who develop COPD have never smoked. Some are predisposed to have this illness through a genetic component. Others were exposed to chemical agents, such as my friends who fought in Vietnam. Exposure to fibreglass and mould can also cause this disease.

When I went for a follow-up appointment to my pulmonary, I had a doctor who was substituting for my regular GP. At one point, he said, *Oh, you must have smoked a lot of cigarettes.* At this point during the conversation, he had no idea I was an ex-smoker and assumed I was because I had COPD. I felt disrespected, and I quickly educated him on how his remarks presented as judgmental and irrelevant and cruel at this point. I am genuinely aware of the part I played within my demise, so I ask those who play the blame and shame game, whether consciously or unconsciously, to please move on because I have.

I learned there are different stages and severities on the COPD spectrum. It is a disease that literally takes my breath away. Walking up or down a staircase is problematic. There are times when I appear not to have a disability at all, and then there are times when the smell of bleach, strong perfume, or vapours from an idling car can choke me. Being in the steam of a shower tends to leave me short of breath, and I tire easily with days when all I can manage is getting out of bed. However, to this point, I never allow myself to stay there because having COPD will not stop me. I have faith that, one day, there will be a cure. Until then, I take each day as it comes and make the most of changes in my world.

The strength and determination of others who refuse to give up inspire me to do better. Many of the friends with COPD I was fortunate to meet from all over the world have moved away from the site where we used to connect and now talk through Facebook and Messenger. Through this illness, I have learned to tune into my inner voice. I am my own advocate when it comes to discussing my conditions with any doctor. My general practitioner, Dr. McKay, respects me enough to ask me about how I would like to proceed, and while he shares his opinions on what course to take, he honours my final say. I no longer do anything when I feel unwell. There is no point. And I surround myself with people who care enough to understand. There are days when I can move mountains and others when my energy and breathing make it too difficult to socialize. I still fly by the seat of my pants into the unknown, but now, I move forward with a bit more caution. I dedicate most of my days to the computer, journaling and writing my memories, and I spend a lot of time on the telephone because I have many children, and most of them call me daily. I always marvel at how much they love me. My life is full in very different ways from the days before the onset of my illnesses.

I do not know what I have done to deserve all the blessings in my life. I am truly humbled by the love that constantly surrounds me. My fifteen-year-old granddaughter tells me all the time,

"Nana, you are never going to die because when you die, you will just keep coming back! You don't do dying well, Nana." I guess she is right; my family is stuck with me.

Through my diagnoses and life with chronic illness, I find solace in my sense of humour and connection with my family.

Chronic Illness Will Never Define me

The more I push myself, the more I create a better life for myself. I often hear from others that they get depressed and are sick of being sick, and I admit that when I was first diagnosed with these illnesses, I became depressed and afraid. I believe I have a degree of PSTD because, to this day, I cannot lie down for an afternoon nap without jerking awake if I feel myself going to sleep. My husband and children worry and do not allow me to stay in the darkness. They push me to walk more, they swim with me in the summer, and they make me laugh. Sure, I have slowed down, but what is the hurry? I am unable to go hiking in the snow, but previous to Covid, I could go for a coffee with friends, and I look forward to when we can all do that again. I also still enjoy walking down to the beach with Drew.

Managing several chronic illnesses has given me a new, fresh perspective on life, feeling grateful for my husband Drew and my eight wonderful children. And I am alive with each day bringing something new! My life is never dull, and even though I wake up some mornings with all sorts of plans in my head, I have learned that my body cannot do everything my head wants to. There are days when it is just too much, but like Pollyanna said, *Tomorrow is another day,* so what we cannot do today may be done the next or even the next. I have learned to listen to my body. I read more, I stress less, and I am back to writing and enjoying life as I have come to know it.

My doctor suggested I throw a kidney specialist into the mix. Why not? I went to my first appointment with Drew to see what the heck all this was about. Low and behold, my kidney function is lower than normal. Go figure. So, my kidneys are monitored with check-ups every three months and annually. So far, my numbers are significantly low but not to the point of needing dialysis yet. Most of my appointments are held on the phone due to pandemic restrictions. At the first appointment, the nurse suggested I speak with a social worker to discuss dialysis, hospice care, end-of-life preparation, and writing a will. All I could say was, *Isn't this a cheery place! In no way am I speaking with someone about preparing to die unless I really am dying.* I also half-jokingly added that I certainly wouldn't without a glass of wine. Drew turned many shades of red.

Since last year I have had cataract surgery, and I receive injections into my eye to stop retinal bleeding. These lovely sessions take place every five months at the cost of 1600 dollars per injection. As stated somewhere in our wedding vows, it is required that Drew *shalt be present to allow me to clench his hand whilst I undergo said torture.* And he does.

I have never felt stronger than when faced with survival. Having a chronic illness with the threat of progression lead me to find my inner strength just as I always have. The trick is that I manage to find passion in my life no matter the adversity. Even though I am ill, I am still on this side of the grass, and I encourage myself and others to accept what has become my new normal, knowing I have the ability to thrive within it. I am still me, the same person who was so easily loved before becoming ill. It is safe to say I do not want to be pitied; I simply want to be understood. I was sad to discover how many people lose their friends when they need them the most. It isn't easy getting to know someone all over again, and I could not accept the new me at first either. Guilt played a large part in this process because I felt I was a burden as I watched my husband take over the work that I thought I should be doing. I could not travel to see my children as I was afraid of being away from my home. Then, later when Covid-19 hit, I was even more restricted. When my children come to visit, I feel bad when they make our meals. I must depend on my husband to take me to my doctor appointments and my children to help me walk.

I hear people say they are pissed as hell after being diagnosed. Why me, why now? There is never an adequate answer, and this is all part of the grieving process. I was able to recognize these feelings early on, and that is the key to moving forward. I know that getting stuck is never healthy and is the time to reach out. Meeting so many warriors with similar conditions online provides the space to share a laugh or two with those who truly understand, which always lightens the load. My life has changed, but I am still me.

I Almost Lost My Marbles…Until I Didn't

Chronic Illness will never define me.
This statue named Expansion is found at
Frind winery in West Kelowna.
After the sculptress, Paige Bradley, first completed it,
she decided she didn't like the statue,
so she broke it into pieces.
Then, she was inspired to reclaim its beauty by putting it
back together again.
I resonate with this, feeling I built a good life after going
through many storms just to have my health
break me into pieces.
I needed to redefine my life and pick up the broken parts.
Through the process of learning to accept who I am now,
I honoured my warrior within.

X

Oh, COVID, You Have Got To Be Kidding

It was an early morning in March 2020 when I turned on my television and saw what all the reporters referred to as *breaking news*. A new virus was spreading worldwide and killing more people globally than any other in modern times. It was and is inconceivable to me that we are experiencing a pandemic of this size without a clear cause and no cure in sight in this day and age.

My first thought was that it was simply a bad flu, and I told myself that our health authorities would be able to get it under control quickly. However, I watched in horror as the number of cases and deaths grew, and I soon realized this was more serious than I previously thought. As world leaders and local politicians spoke of closing down schools, businesses, and churches for our protection, I became aware that having four chronic illnesses put me at extremely high risk for not surviving this life-threatening virus called COVID-19. I had a vivid memory of what it was like recovering on a ventilator and how lucky I was to survive. Would I be as fortunate a second time?

As Drew and I drove through our small town on a Sunday during the first wave of this pandemic, it looked like a ghost town - eerie and surreal. The restaurants and shops that usually bustled on the weekends were closed down. There were very few people out for a walk along the beach boardwalk – typically, it was filled with people passing each other, chatting, walking their dogs, and sharing conversations while sipping coffee. Our children's playground was empty, prohibiting anyone from entering with tape surrounding its perimeter. I felt sad, and a sense of despair began setting in.

My granddaughter provided the lens that the impact of closing schools down has had on young children. Nothing can replace the freedom to play with friends. As an only child, she was especially lonely and sad. It was hard to explain to a six-year-old why she couldn't have a playdate. There were many times I wished I lived closer to her, but it didn't matter because we were not allowed to visit one another. So, she and I connected in a new way on Skype. I knew I could not replace her friends, but I wanted to make sure she knew I was sending her love. In return, she sent me and Grandpop Drew artwork that I display proudly in my office. I greatly miss her hugs.

Over the years, I had somewhat gotten used to being alone while my husband went away to work for extended periods, but the first time he prepared to leave for three weeks during lockdown, I wondered how I would survive this. So, I turned to and experienced the incredible support our small town put in place for those considered to be vulnerable. The government asked us to stay at home, and in gratitude, I watched how our community rallied. Volunteers from Peachland Wellness picked up groceries for people who could not safely get out. Medications were delivered free of charge, and for the most part, doctor's appointments were held online or by phone. Nothing skipped a beat, and things remained the same and yet different in how they were delivered.

I was extremely lonely, being someone who thrives on human connection. It is how I maintain a sense of balance, and without it, I was moving into a depressed state of being. I then decided I needed to find a way to go along for the ride in a quickly changing world. I found different ways to connect, starting with myself. If I was going to survive this new way, I decided to look inside myself and bring back my fighting spirit. I began writing my memoir, realizing I needed to reconnect with myself to get through the challenges I was facing. So I started back at my childhood and moved through the different adventures that life gave me along the way. Being a lover of writing and a huge fan of history, I delved into my background, learning more and more about myself. Writing my story has been quite cathartic, taking the time and creating the space to become more in touch with who I am from the inside and out. My perception of myself is that I am a warrior, and for the most part, I am. Then, other times, I see myself as a big broken mess. I think I am a bit of both in a good way, and when I feel the latter, I realize I am out of touch with my reality in how I think and act. This is when I embrace myself with compassion. The road has been long and rough, getting to this point, and slowly but surely, I continue moving forward.

 I always believed in the importance of being kind to others, as well as to myself. I practice more self-care than ever before, waking up with a cup of tea and slowing my life down through journaling. Sometimes, I go down to my happy place at the beach. I love to put on music and dance. These are things that take me to a place of calm when my mind seems to wander into chaos. Having gratitude also allows me to remain hopeful and connected to all that is positive in the world - they always appear when I take the time to notice.

 Years ago, my great friend Catherine encouraged me to meditate, and my oldest daughter swears by it. However, it proved to be difficult when my children were young as I sat crossed-legged on my bed, and inevitably, the knocking would start on the bedroom door, *Mom where are my soccer cleats; can you drive me to so and so's house, and the list went on.* Over time, I gave up. Now, years later, with more time on my hands, I have come back to try it again. I listen to calming music and shut myself down for a few moments. I even have an Apple watch that tells me when to breath. I call it Norton the Nag because it tells me when to stand, when to breathe, and when to exercise. One night, in front of my children, it even told me that it was time to go to bed. I'm not sure what button I, inadvertently, pushed to make it do all that, but I believe Norton may be possessed - if I had wanted someone to tell me what to do all the time, I would have kept my ex! I remember when I first got my Apple phone. I was not used to using it and somehow got Siri after pushing several buttons. I was so frustrated with Siri popping up for the zillionth time, trying to help me, so I told her to *bugger off.* She replied, *It would have been more polite if you had said, please go away.* I jumped out of my skin, threw my cell phone down, and just stared at it. After I had collected myself, I called my oldest daughter, who said her sides ached for days from laughing so hard.

I have progressed to downloading the Calm app, so I feel I am moving in the right direction... maybe? I love the idea of running a bubble bath and hopping into the tub with a glass of wine and reading. However, I am not all that coordinated, and I discovered that wine glasses break, so I now stick to the bubble bath alone.

As summer approached, the stay-at-home order lifted in British Columbia. It appeared to be business as usual with a film company and its crew coming to Peachland to shoot a Christmas movie on our pier. I was able to have my children visit the lake for a weekend. Even though restaurants opened, it was suggested we remain in small groups of family members only and limit contact with others through social distancing.

I watched the beaches fill with local families, and many tourists were evident in the downtown area. I wondered how safe this really was. The government did not put restrictions on travel, so it led me to believe it must not be considered an at-risk situation. Playgrounds were opened at last, and I saw so many happy little faces enjoying the swings and slides while interacting with their friends once again. It filled my heart with joy, knowing my youngest granddaughter could once again play and be a child.

Summer turned into fall, and COVID case numbers were on the rise once again. The politicians and the Health Authority in BC allowed schools to reopen as they saw what I witnessed with my granddaughter. They determined that the adverse mental health effects on our children far outweighed the need to close schools. I was happy about this, yet also concerned about the increase in numbers. An order was put into place, mandating wearing a mask inside any public place. The first time I went into the grocery store wearing a mask, I felt like I was entering another world. And maybe I was. Having COPD, masks present a challenge for me. If I am wearing one for any length of time, I become short of breath, and sometimes, also dizzy. However, I prefer the mask over a ventilator. There is a lot of controversy over wearing masks, but I believe they do reduce the spread. I am happy to be part of the solution rather than part of the problem. Nothing feels normal to me. That is because what we perceived as our normal before this pandemic arrived has all but disappeared. Will times ever return to what we had before? I don't know. But I have faith we will come out of this as we do all storms, albeit somewhat changed and more resilient. Perhaps this is our opportunity to see a real need for change.

Fall saw the re-implementation of restrictions, along with a few more. Once again, restaurants were hit hard with complete shutdowns in some provinces. In BC, the Health Authorities limited the number of diners to be within your bubble. This meant that only immediate family living together in one home could dine out together with a maximum number of six people per table. Christmas travel to my children's homes was out of the question, and there was an order that stated only family members of the same household could gather for the holidays. All this meant that, for the very first time in a very long time, my children and I could not gather in one place for Christmas dinner. This made me incredibly sad. Christmas has always been a significant celebration in my family, and it looked very different last year. Some of my children even spent this special day alone. It was hard, but somehow, we got through it. Fortunately for me, Drew's shift wasn't starting until the first part of January, so I did not spend the holidays by myself.

I look back at some other changes that evolved from the pandemic. There were positives to take away from a changed season. One of my sons bought donations to charities as Christmas gifts instead of presents. He bought me a donation to the Battered Women's Shelter in Vancouver, and it touched my heart in such a profoundly appreciative way. Drew and I adopted a family who did not have enough money for toys or a Christmas dinner. It was time I paid it forward on behalf of all of us. I also gave money to homeless youth through Mamas for Mamas.[9] So, it felt different but in a good way. I believed we all recognized what we had and gratefully passed on blessings to others. By looking inside ourselves, we were able to reflect on our fortunate lives and help others.

We learned that vaccines were approved for distribution

---

[1] Ibid

in December 2020, and they would be in our arms soon. Collectively, most of the world shared a sigh of relief. I believed there was an end in sight, and everything would be okay now, but trailing behind me was fear that life would always be this way. Sadly, the variants spread more easily and are as deadly as the primary COVID-19 virus. BC continued strict orders on gatherings, churches remained closed, and restrictions on non-essential travel were put in place. Only restaurants with patios could remain open. I heard it was even more severe in other provinces with absolute lockdowns in place. All this left me frightened again, and I began questioning how effective the first vaccines would be. On April 23rd, 2021, I received my first shot and Drew got his four days later. I am unclear if it will protect me against the variants and what the side effects will be if any. I have deduced that I require more clarity to achieve balance and experience less trepidation. I was fearful about the vaccine and its possible side effects, yet I surrendered to it. My side effects were mild, lasting only a couple of days with low energy, a headache and feeling dizzy upon standing; Drew had none at all. I consider this much better than the alternative of enduring COVID and possibly dying.

I found myself stuck in sadness, worry, and I was unable to sleep throughout this pandemic. My doctor recommended possible helpful counselling and medication remedies. I never really thought I had anxiety until COVID-19 entered the world. Counselling has been a difficult road for me as the counsellor in me tries to support the therapist, so I chose to take medication to help me sleep. The jury is still out on this medication because I sleep better but feel groggy during the day.

When I see protesters in blatant non-compliance with public health orders, I feel discouraged. One weekend, Drew, my daughter and I went to downtown Kelowna, and we drove by what the participants call a *freedom protest*. I can understand and have some degree of compassion for them as I recognize their fear and frustration as normal reactions to what is happening at the moment. I know they believe that their rights are being violated. I wish I could sit down with those who choose to party in large groups on our beaches and protest in groups unmasked, laughing in the face of social distancing. I would share with them that I empathize that they are tired of staying at home. I was young once too, and I thought I was invincible. But I wish they would choose to see another perspective; the viewpoint of the more vulnerable and more likely to die.

I would ask them to consider taking the precautions asked of them for the greater good. We all have a right to our freedom and to protest peacefully, but right now may not be the best time to gather. Thinking about everyone before acting is all I ask. These are not normal times, and not complying with what our health officials are recommending could create a potentially lethal situation for many, continuing to take more lives. Prolonging the virus by putting fuel to its fire will create *super spreading* and ruin the economy even further. This pandemic will last longer, and you will unknowingly put me and many others at greater risk. There is a real possibility that I would die from this virus. Ask any health care worker entrenched in the front lines just how real the virus is. They work endless hours in situations that no one would ever wish to be in. They watch people pass away and make calls to their next of kin daily. I have hope that this is not the outcome you wish for, especially if there is any chance that your choice could make a difference.

One of my friends is a nurse, and she told me that those who refuse to wear a mask or believe this virus is a hoax has never had to zip up a body bag or make that one call to tell a relative their loved one did not make it. She also shared that it is not uncommon to find one of her colleagues on the covid ward in a closet weeping out of sheer pain and frustration because of what they experience during each of their shifts. It saddens me that people like my friend work to the point of exhaustion only to feel mocked and ridiculed. They are the real heroes and also victims caused by the additional mental health toll during this unimaginable time. Mental illness is a serious side effect that is an increasingly growing concern for all ages. Another friend who works as a nurse in the public health sector told me that episodes including alcoholism, drug abuse, and accidental overdoses are severe consequences and are clearly at an all-time high.

    I am certain that this pandemic is bringing out paranoia in a lot of people. The fear is real. At this point, no one can tell us when or how this will end. I fight the thought that this is our new normal, yet part of me wonders if this is indeed a fact, given I can't see the end. I think the scariest thing about COVID-19 is that we are still learning what it is composed of and how to fight it. To date, there are no fast and proven answers. I think it is difficult to keep hope alive when the virus continues to mutate with an abundance of variables, and solutions are few and far between. But try we must, or we will all be on the brink of losing our marbles.

    I am finding that choices are being made based on how much risk an individual is comfortable taking. For me, I would say I take calculated risks. For example, my daughter, who lives alone, comes over for Sunday dinners. I make one weekly grocery trip, choosing not to visit large retail stores or the mall to avoid crowds. When in a store, I wear a mask and do my best to social distance. To get some fresh air and a lot of fun, my daughter and I take her dog to the off-leash doggie park, where there is lots of room for everyone to spread out.

I like to keep busy while Drew is away to distract me from being alone, so I learned to make various homemade soups, which I am sure my children are surprised about because I used to cook out of boxes and serve premade meals whenever possible. Carrot, turkey noodle, and ginger squash soup are among my favourites. The other reason I make these when Drew is away is that I make a heck of a mess of our kitchen, and I freeze them to eat when he gets home. This surprisingly allows me to put my creativity to use, and I even started to bake muffins and cookies. I found lots of recipes that allow me to substitute sugar with stevia, a plant-based sweetener. This means I can eat the treats I bake.

My favourite times are when Drew comes home from camp and we go on long drives together. We stop to take pictures and have lunch on outdoor patios. These outings provide some beautiful experiences that keep my mental health in check. I work every day at fighting thoughts of fear and loneliness. Being a bit of a social butterfly, I miss one-on-one connection with family and friends. I practice gratitude and kindness every day of my life. This journey is one in which I know each of us needs to be able to connect – it may be in a different way than we are used to, but we still need to connect. During lockdowns, it made me incredibly sad to see patients in long-term care homes alone without family allowed to visit them. My heart ached to discover the high mortality rate at facilities. Many residents did not understand and felt abandoned.

Just lately, both Drew and I received the blessing of being reunited with old friends. My neighbours had a social distancing gathering in our parking lot. We followed all the rules and sat on our lawn chairs, sharing friendships and conversations that otherwise may not have happened. They say *necessity is the mother of invention*, and I believe that to be true.

As a mother, I worry about my children all the time. It is hard not to when you can't be with them. Just because they are all grown up does not mean I will ever stop thinking about them. I know worrying is ineffective and a total waste of time, yet I still fall prey to it. Drew works up in Nunavut and flies back and forth. To me, this means he is at a greater risk of contracting COVID than I am. He gets tested twice when he is in camp, yet it is always in the back of my mind that he may not be safe. I recognize that these are dark places to go and not worthwhile emotions, and I work hard to accept what I cannot change. Having had his first dose of the vaccine helps me feel a little better. Writing in my journal every morning brings awareness to how I feel and clarity of my thoughts; I fight to let go of things that are out of my control, and yet, during this period of my life, I struggle to avoid a negative mindset.

But then, I go through stages when I think there must be purpose amidst all this change! And if there is a purpose, it is up to me to determine what it is. I have noticed young families who have this unprecedented chance to step away from solitary activities such as engaging on social media, watching television, and playing video games to spend quality time with each other. As a child, I loved going outdoors and dancing in the rain. Unfortunately, I find that our overly busy world has lost our spunk, our passion for thinking outside the box. I always find comfort and solace when stepping back and counting my blessings. Throughout my life and my most difficult times, this simple act has served me well as I find joy in simpler things and feel hope for a future full of promise. Consciously being kind, remaining calm, and vibrating positivity are the intentions I choose as I continue to move through this storm. I am a firm believer in the saying *what goes around comes around*, so I am constantly aware of my actions. I know this is hard with a rough road ahead of us, but if we pull together instead of pulling apart, I strongly trust that we will make it through this time of upheaval and unrest.

One of the sweetest gifts I received was from a woman in Peachland. People visiting the online site I was on said they were sick of the letters in the mail they received from religious groups and politicians. I half-jokingly stated that I would love to get a letter from anyone. Unbeknownst to me, a lady who worked at the insurance company we use in town saw the post and sent me a wonderful card with a big smile on it.

Unfortunately, right or wrong, not every day is hopeful, but something like this brings me that little bit of hope, inspiring me to carry on.

It is now the end of April 2021. As we enter what they refer to as our third wave, I see case numbers rising again, and the number of deaths amongst younger people is at frightening levels. Deep in my soul, I feel that the only way to get through this successfully is to stay home and isolate. It breaks my heart that I cannot see my children. I want so much to wrap my arms around them and keep the monsters away like I did when they were younger. This global epidemic has a roller coaster effect; we just get ahead, and then, we fall back again. There is once again another shortage of vaccines predicted as the flow from other countries has hit a temporary pause. Heading into May, our province has put higher restrictions on travel. No one is allowed to travel, to cross from one health authority – once again, my children cannot come to visit me. With all of us having our first vaccine, we had tentative plans to get together soon. However, they are not allowed to come by penalty of a hefty fine. We will wait and do the right thing because it is better than the alternative.

My frustration lies with the lack of enforcement around the orders. Even the police in Vancouver do not seemingly appear to want to get involved by shutting down the protests or the flagrant unlawful actions of some individuals. For example, one restaurant owner held a protest against the shutdown of indoor dining by holding a rally outside. She stated that she could not afford to shut down her indoor space because she has four children to raise. Although I understand the extreme financial hardship all business owners are enduring, I cannot imagine those children being told that their mother became a victim of COVID-19.

My son was travelling home from work on the sea bus not long ago, and another passenger boarded without a mask. My son asked him to please don his mask, and he refused, saying he didn't believe in masks. My son pointed this out to the sea bus authority, who stated that they did not like conflict, so they would not enforce the mandatory order. Other passengers then ridiculed my son for causing a disturbance.

The world is in quite a state, and there are moments when I simply want to go to bed, pull the covers over my head, and awaken to a world returned to some semblance of normalcy. This will go down as one of the darkest times in history, and it is more important than ever that we help one another put out the fires in our lives. Whether we endure an emotional or financial setback or both, we are all managing turmoil, and many feel alone. Yet, I believe that together we can combat the side effects that COVID presents.

On any given day, I move through a gamut of emotions - I can be happy, sad, anxious, or peaceful, but I never experience them simultaneously. I do not know what tomorrow will bring, and I don't know if there will even be one. I am manifesting that I will hug my children again one day in the near future and hold my grandchildren tightly. I hope and pray this to be true as I end my story, not knowing how I will cope in the days ahead, but just that I must. This is the only way I know how as I, once again, tap into my lifeline of resilience. I wish everyone out there to find the patience and strength to continue fighting and experience the awareness necessary to remain optimistic about the bright future we all deserve. Amidst all this chaos, I am deeply thankful to all who put their lives on the line each day to keep us out of harm's way. Namaste.

Oh, COVID, You Have Got To Be Kidding

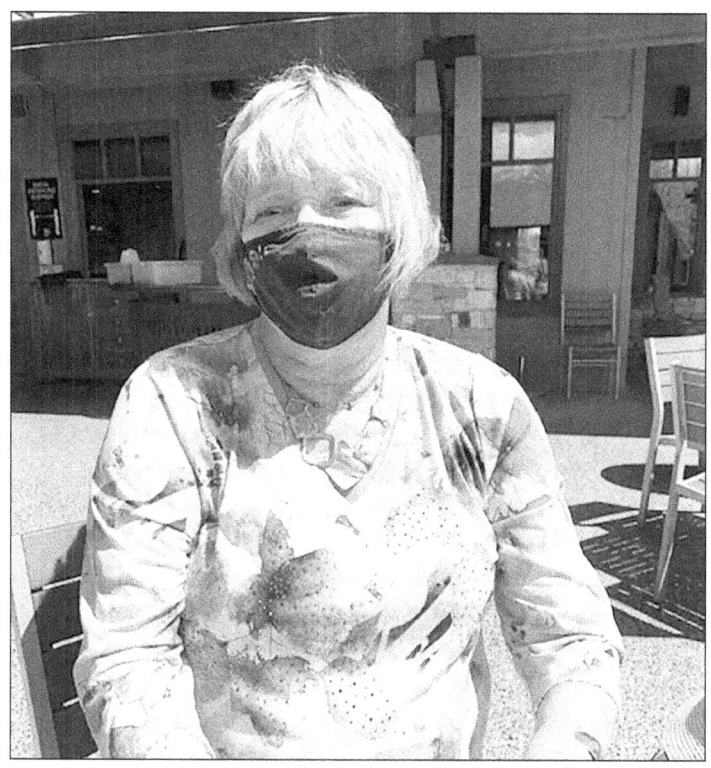

Oh, COVID, You Have Got to be Kidding!!
Wearing my mandatory mask in indoor places.
My daughter and I were at the Twin Eagles Golf and Country Club in West Kelowna, BC enjoying a glass of wine on their patio. We were allowed to be without a mask when sitting at our table which was social distanced.
However, we had to wear it when walking away from our table for any reason.
Be responsible. Be mindful.
Our lives depend upon it.

About Dorri Warga

Dorri Warga was motivated to write her story through the joyous self-awakening she found while discovering her truth... her authentic self. In writing her memoirs, she allowed herself to reflect on how the universe works, providing opportunities in places of darkness — within those moments came a breakthrough to a life filled with enthusiastically embracing opportunities.

Dorri uses her sense of humour to create the energy of connection with others. By doing so, she hopes the load will be lighter for the lives she touches, especially during this time with COVID-19.

Her life was not always easy. In fact, at times, it was downright scary. Yet, by remaining optimistic and trusting in the universe, she found ways to cope and thrive. Dorri believes that all storms and challenges present keys to moving forward. This is what enabled her to push through with the positive perception she had.

One of the incredible *aha* moments in her life came when she recognized that all the name-calling and negative emotions that sought to crush her spirit were just noise — that the real person inside, the true identifying self, remained steadfast. At that moment, she knew she had the power to become who she sought to be.

Throughout her career, Dorri worked with a diverse population of people and led her groups with deep empathy and an understanding of the issues directly related to them. As a Life and Career Coach, she committed to leading and not teaching. The respect she received in return provided her with feelings of appreciation, and it warmed her heart.

Over the duration of six years, Dorri was diagnosed with four chronic illnesses. This was an adjustment, and she was, once again, called upon to reach inside to find her warrior spirit. She now encourages others with chronic illnesses to find the sun where shadows fall.

Dorri has eight wonderful children and was a single parent for a considerable period of their lives. She met Drew and married him in 2005. They live in Peachland, British Columbia, where she finds peace and comfort at her happy place, the beach.

Rattlesnake Island

www.ingramcontent.com/pod-product-compliance
Lightning Source LLC
Chambersburg PA
CBHW072155100526
44589CB00015B/2236